Take

Time

*for*

Your

Life

# Take Time *for* Your Life

A PERSONAL COACH'S
SEVEN-STEP PROGRAM
FOR CREATING THE LIFE
YOU WANT

**Cheryl Richardson**

*Broadway Books  New York*

**BROADWAY**

A hardcover edition of this book was published in 1998 by Broadway Books.

TAKE TIME FOR YOUR LIFE. Copyright © 1999 by Cheryl Richardson. All rights reserved. Printed in the United States of America. No part of this book may be reproduced or transmitted in any form or by any means, electronic or mechanical, including photocopying, recording, or by any information storage and retrieval system, without written permission from the publisher. For information, address Broadway Books, a division of Random House, Inc., 1540 Broadway, New York, NY 10036.

Broadway Books titles may be purchased for business or promotional use or for special sales. For information, please write to: Special Markets Department, Random House, Inc., 1540 Broadway, New York, NY 10036.

BROADWAY BOOKS and its logo, a letter B bisected on the diagonal, are trademarks of Broadway Books, a division of Random House, Inc.

First trade paperback edition published 1999.

The Library of Congress has cataloged the hardcover edition as:
Richardson, Cheryl.
Take time for your life: a personal coach's seven-step program for creating the life you want / Cheryl Richardson. — 1st ed.
        p.   cm.
    1. Conduct of life.   2. Quality of life.   I. Title.
            BF637.C5R53    1998
        158.1—dc21                98-20982
                        CIP

Author's note: The names and details of the coaching examples provided in this book have been changed when necessary to respect the confidentiality of the coaching relationships.

ISBN 0-7679-0207-6

00   01   02   03   04   10   9   8

———

*This book is dedicated to my husband, Michael,*
*the most loving and honorable man I have ever known.*

# CONTENTS

---

# ACKNOWLEDGMENTS

Throughout my life I have been blessed to have shared a connection with so many people who have supported me both personally and professionally. The love and wisdom I've received has been channeled into this book. Because the list would fill a book itself, and because I'm so afraid of forgetting a single soul, let me say up front that I am deeply grateful to each and every one of you for your support.

Every writer needs a guardian angel to silence the critics that sit on her shoulder while she writes. Marilyn Abraham has been that angel. Without her guidance, encouragement, sense of humor, and seasoned skill, this book would never have been written. Thank you, Marilyn, from the bottom of my heart. (And a special thanks to Maggie Lichtenberg, who brought us together and offered her support whenever I needed it.)

My dear friend and soul sister Max Dilley, who ate sushi with me whenever I craved it, reminded me to keep the faith, believed in me when I didn't believe in myself, and always knew the perfect thing to say. Thank you, Max, especially for the prayer in the airport.

Many thanks to my colleagues who have helped pioneer this profession including: my dear friend Stephen Cluney; fellow author Laura Berman Fortgang; members of the Coaches Council; Sandy Vilas, president of Coach University, and all the students I have been so lucky to learn from; Steve Shull, Vance Caesar, Ed Shea, Ellen Wingard, and Jeff Raim, who took over the leadership of the International Coach Federation which allowed me to write this book—you've done an outstanding job! I'd like to thank my first coach and mentor, Thomas Leonard, the man who put the coaching profession on the map, for his wisdom, support, and introduction to the concept of extreme self-care. His coaching concepts are not only reflected throughout this book, but have had a profound influence on the woman I've become and the way I live my life.

A heartfelt thanks to Pat Rogers, whose unwavering love, support, and guidance has taught me to truly be myself; Niravi Payne, who challenged me to find my voice and step out fully into the world; and to my own coach, Shirley Anderson (Coach Miami), whose friendship and love held the vision of my work when I was blinded by fear (and deadlines).

A special thanks to Joan Oliver, editor of *New Age* magazine, whose friendship and support was there from the beginning; to Marguerite Rigoglioso, a terrific writer with passion and sensibility; to David Thorne, a mentor, friend, and true supporter of my work; to Lama Surya Das, a fellow writer and friend who helped me walk through the "publishing machine" with patience and open eyes.

I am lucky to have had Lauren Marino at Broadway Books as my editor. Lauren is one of the best—smart, thorough, committed, and always available. Thank you for challenging me to find my voice on the page and for editing with the reader's heart in mind.

To my publicist at Broadway, Debbie Stier—who, I'm convinced, can move mountains with a touch of her hand. She's the kind of person that you pray to have on your team. To my agent, Ashley Carroll, whose enthusiasm, guts, responsiveness, and sense of humor make it a joy to work together. To David Smith, president of D.H.S. Literary Agency, whose commitment and support of this project went above and beyond the call of duty. And thanks to Sally Jaskold for her fine copyediting skills.

My deep gratitude goes to my virtual assistant, partner, and dear friend, Stacy Brice, who takes care of my personal and professional life so completely. Finding you was like discovering the most perfect diamond in the world—I am eternally grateful.

To my family, all thirteen of them, who have given me the perfect gifts I've needed to live a life that I love. A special thanks to my sisters, Lisa and Michelle, two terrific virtual assistants who helped compile the resource section of this book. A very special thanks to my mom, who continuously called my voice mail and sang little songs to encourage me as I've built a successful career, and who validated my intuitive abilities at an early age, teaching me that intuition is not only an important tool for living a spiritually guided life but also for building a successful business. And to my dad, thank you so much for the life lessons that have shaped the woman I've become including: Never forget where you came from, share your wealth, and always take the time to show you care. And to my new in-laws, Pat and Curt Gerrish, every bride should be so lucky to have new parents like you!

Thank you to Gay Schoene, Linda Novotny, Peter Valaskatgis, Ania O'Connor, and Dr. Jonathan Berg—all very gifted healers.

And a big thank-you to Kelly O'Brien, whose unconditional love started me on my path of healing and growth—she was the first angel I recognized.

And to you, my clients, I am blessed beyond measure to have shared in your lives. Thank you for your patience while I wrote this book and for your trust, honesty, and willingness to take action. You have made my journey a true adventure. This book is a culmination of all I have learned from the thousands of private conversations that I've been privileged to share over the last fifteen years.

And, finally, to my husband, Michael Gerrish who, while up against his own book deadline, supported me every step of the way. No woman has ever been more lucky. You give new meaning to the term "soulmate."

# Introduction: What

# Coaching Can

# Do for You

———

Would you like to change your life? Do you long for a sense of community? More time for yourself? Would you like to take better care of your health, reduce stress, and create more balance in your life? Well, you're not alone. More and more people are tired of the fast-paced, frenzied "information age" and are interested in higher-quality lives—lives in which they have more time for themselves and their relationships, more energy to invest in their emotional, physical, and spiritual well-being.

Whether you're a corporate executive working sixty hours a week, a single parent trying to raise a family, or someone who's tired of feeling stressed out and pressed for time, you have a choice about how to live your life. You can step back, reevaluate your priorities, and make a conscious decision about the future you'd like to create. How do you make such a decision? Where do you turn when you decide to improve the quality of your life?

When your body is out of shape and you need help getting fit or losing weight, you hire a personal trainer. Wouldn't it be great if you could do this for all other parts of your life? Well, now you can. With the help of a "personal coach," you can shape up your life and overcome the obstacles that get in the way of living a life that you love. In a sense, you can hire a "personal trainer for your soul."

When people hear that I'm a coach, the first question they inevitably ask is: "What sport?" Once I tell them that I'm not an athletic coach and that I coach people to create lives that they love, they wonder how coaching is different from therapy. It's understandable that most people would confuse the two—therapy is the closest model we have to this new profession called coaching. But the two are very different.

Coaching is not about processing your emotional history or diagnosing and treating mental health issues. Coaching is action oriented, with a focus on a client's current life and plans for the future; although therapy deals with a client's current life, the focus is usually on the past and the healing of emotional wounds. There can be overlap between coaching and therapy, and a well-trained, experienced coach should know when a client needs therapy instead of coaching. Because of this, I've developed relationships with experienced, licensed professionals, and it's not uncommon for us to refer clients to each other.

There is a growing need for more than what therapy provides. In therapy, clients may talk about the changes they'd like to make in their lives, but the "how to" and the resources are often missing. Yet such information is critical to my clients' success. Clients want someone to help them design a new life. They want a guide who can anticipate the obstacles on the path to this new life and help navigate around them. They want a partner who will remind them of their greatness when they forget, give them the tools to get unstuck, and challenge them to take action in spite of their fears. This need is now being met by personal coaches.

The need for coaching became evident to me while I was working as a tax consultant more than fifteen years ago. The time spent with clients was often very personal, requiring an intimate look into their lives. Typically, we'd talk not only about their finances (income, spending habits, and debt) but also about their medical history, family goals, and career plans. The questions they asked often concerned decisions that needed to be made about relocation, relationship conflicts, business dilemmas, or the challenge of balancing work and family. This led to longer conversations about life in general.

Although tax consulting can be a straightforward, "just the facts, ma'am," kind of job, my practice developed in a different direction. Year after year, in addition to their tax folders, clients brought me their life stories, wanting my advice and support. They needed a sounding board, an objective listener who could provide a fresh perspective. I learned how to create an environment in which people could feel comfortable and safe enough to talk about their lives freely.

In private, they would share with me their fears and concerns. Business owners, afraid of losing clients if they raised their fees, would let their own well-being suffer instead. Corporate employees, needing to support their families, struggled with how to handle political issues at work or the insensitivity of bosses.

Together we found solutions to the problems that were causing them stress. Sometimes, simply hearing an objective perspective would make all the difference in the world. Other times, finding the right language to communicate their needs allowed them to get unstuck and take action. Most important, knowing that they were not alone and that others grappled with the same kind of issues provided them with comfort and much needed support.

Over time I became less interested in preparing people's tax returns and more interested in helping them prioritize their lives to spend more time with their families or fulfill a secret dream, like starting a business or having a child. I decided to stop providing my tax consulting services and start responding full-time to the greater concerns of my clients. I began to do this by holding workshops called "Secrets of Success" and speaking to groups about everything from goal setting to relationship-building strategies. People were relieved to find someone who could help them overcome obstacles to better their lives. One thing was clear—there was a need for "life planning" but there was no one to turn to. This need for objective guidance and support has spawned the profession of coaching.

Many people from all walks of life are turning to coaches to help them build better lives. The reasons may vary, but the bottom line is always the same—they want to improve the quality of their lives in some way. My client Shirley is a good example.

Shirley is the vice president of sales for a fast-growing biotech company. By most standards, she has reached a considerable level of success—she earns six figures, shares a beautiful lakeside home with her husband, and is a recognized leader in her field. But Shirley doesn't feel successful; she feels exhausted. Her day begins at 6 A.M. with a trip to the gym and continues nonstop until 8 or 9 at night. Most days—among the endless meetings, phone calls, and social engagements—she finds herself dreaming of a different life, a life that includes more time for herself, less stress, and a chance to express her creativity. Shirley's tired of living her best life in her head.

My client Joseph is a corporate employee who's already been the victim of downsizing and is afraid that he's headed in the same direction again. Joseph goes to work every day filled with anxiety, fearful that each day may be his last. After giving ten good years to his employer, an architectural firm, he knows that the marketplace has changed, and the company is now involved in restructuring. With mounting debt and one child headed for college, Joseph can't afford to miss a day of work, let alone lose his job.

And then there's my client Norman, the owner of a successful financial investment firm. Norman travels at least twice a month to visit clients scattered throughout the country. He has eight sales associates who call him at all hours of the day and night and a fiancée who complains that they never spend quality time together. Norman feels like life is rushing by at lightning speed, and he's starting to get nervous. He jokingly admits that he needs to stop and get a life, but he can't seem to slow down.

Joseph, Shirley, and Norman are caught in a trap. Each has come up against the kind of obstacles that prevent most people from taking control of their lives. For example, Shirley has no time for her life and feels frustrated by all the demands placed on her. She struggles to carve out time for the things she really wants to do—like taking a class and working in her garden. What's stopping her is an inability to put herself first. Shirley needs permission to make her self-care a top priority over anything else.

Joseph, on the other hand, appears to need another job, fast, but a new job is only part of the solution. The source of Joseph's problem is his vulnerable financial state. His credit card balances are maxed out, his mortgage is too high, and his family spends more than they make. To truly be in charge of his career, Joseph needs to invest in his financial health.

As for Norman, he may need to learn new skills to manage his employees better, but the first order of business is for him to manage himself. He's running on adrenaline and must learn how to slow down and use healthier sources of fuel.

As a personal coach, it's my job to listen carefully, beneath the symptoms of a situation, for the source of the problem. If you're feeling exhausted, a better diet or exercise program will certainly help, but you may first need to identify and eliminate what's draining you. Or, if you're constantly undermined by people who criticize you or put you down, setting boundaries can make a difference, but sometimes you need to trade in those unsupportive relationships for more life-enhancing ones. If work has taken over your life, finding a way to manage your time won't solve the problem. Instead, you'll need to manage yourself, get your priorities straight, and focus your attention on what really matters. Most important, if you long to live a more authentic life, one that reflects your values and desires, then you must give your spiritual well-being a more prominent place in your daily life.

Over the last fifteen years I've coached hundreds of clients who have wanted to significantly change their lives. During weekly telephone meetings, I listen carefully as clients talk about what they want and don't want in their lives. Over time, I've identified seven com-

mon obstacles that consistently prevent people from living lives that
they love:

1. **You think "selfish" is a dirty word.** You have a hard
   time putting your needs before others and often end up
   feeling frustrated and resentful about the commitments you
   make.

2. **Your schedule does not reflect your priorities.** You find
   yourself exhausted at the end of the day without enough
   time left for the things that are most important to you.

3. **You feel drained by people, places, and things.** Your
   life feels like one long list of things to do that never seem
   to get completed. Your office still needs organizing, your
   home may be full of clutter, or you may feel drained by a
   friend or family member's constant complaints.

4. **You feel trapped by money.** You're tired of not being
   able to make the choices you want because of financial
   constraints. You may be saddled with unwanted debt,
   struggling to make ends meet, or feeling unsatisfied with
   the way you spend your money.

5. **Adrenaline has become your main source of fuel.**
   You're constantly running from one appointment to the
   next. You'd like to relax but you can't seem to slow down.
   Peace of mind seems like an impossible goal.

6. **You're missing a supportive community in your life.**
   You feel isolated or disconnected from others and long to
   share a deeper connection with a community of like-
   minded people.

7. **Your spiritual well-being gets last place in your busy
   life.** You'd like to spend consistent time in meditation,
   prayer, practicing yoga, or other forms of spiritual self-
   care, but life keeps getting in the way.

These are the seven blocks that, when given time and attention, can
easily be turned around. Overcoming these obstacles is the focus of

this book. If you're willing to work hard and invest your time (which this book will help you find!) and energy in this process, I promise you, your life will change dramatically. You can make the shift and put yourself in charge of how you live your life.

You can live a life you love, and I'd like to show you how.

## THE COACHING PARTNERSHIP

The coaching relationship is a partnership between two equals. My relationship with clients is based on the belief that they are smart, mature, and capable people who want support in articulating and achieving their goals. I provide this support and direction in three basic ways:

- I ask provocative questions. I rely on the inner wisdom of my clients to provide important insight into what is needed to plan the next step.
- I give direct advice and information. Drawing on personal experience as well as my work with others, I provide a variety of expertise and resources. This helps clients to avoid the mistakes that others have made.
- I provide the focus and structure of ongoing support needed to stay in action. I celebrate clients' successes, hold their hands through difficult periods, and act as a steward for the lives they most want. I'm their partner, and my only agenda is their success.

Since my early years as a tax consultant, I've learned a great deal about coaching others. My formal training as a coach, my life experience, and, most important, my clients, have taught me a lot about what people want and what gets in their way. Although this kind of experience and training is important, equally important is my commitment to model a high-quality life. I've grappled with the same issues my clients are dealing with. I've worked ridiculous hours, built a successful business, made plenty of mistakes in relationships, and paid little attention to my health. Over the last several years, I've used the process in this book to improve my own life. I know it works. I've made the changes that allow me to live exactly as I want to live. My life is a work in progress, and, unlike a therapist, sharing my own personal experience is part of the coaching relationship.

Clients generally decide to work with me because they're ready to make significant changes. They may want to change careers, downsize or upgrade their lives, fulfill a secret dream, or slow down and spend more time and energy on what really matters to them. We start the coaching process with an expectation to spend a minimum of three months working together. However, once we get started and they experience the power of this unique partnership, they often stay much longer.

The initial process of coaching is like building any important relationship. As we spend time getting to know each other, a sense of trust is built that allows clients to tell the truth about their lives. To facilitate this process I ask clients to write a life story that chronicles the significant events of their lives and includes any present-day challenges and frustrations. This information gives me a good idea of where the client has been, what's draining their energy, and which obstacles are causing them the most trouble.

In the beginning many clients tell me that they can't afford to live a life they love. I tell them they can't afford not to. The excuses seem real and insurmountable—their cost of living is too high, so they stay at unfulfilling jobs; they're exhausted with the pace of life and lack the energy needed to make a change; they're too old or too young; it's too soon; it's too late. The most crippling excuse of all is they believe they are victims of circumstance, powerless to change their lives.

## YOUR LIFE, YOUR CHOICE

Making the decision to change your life starts by making a personal choice. Too often we get caught up in all there is to do and forget that we're the ones running the show. It's easy to understand why. The high cost of living often requires two incomes to raise a family. Layoffs continue, encouraging employees to work long hours in the hopes of ensuring job security; and the "the more you make, the more you spend" mentality makes it hard for people of all income levels to make ends meet. This perception of reality makes a high-quality life seem impossible. But don't let this reality fool you. Sometimes, as in Marsha's case, the smallest change can make the biggest difference.

Marsha was a single mom trying to manage a household, a full-time job, and two kids. She was stressed to the breaking point. Fed up, she thought that becoming her own boss would give her the relief she desired. Marsha yearned for the flexibility and freedom she imagined this would bring. The classic "supermom," Marsha was strong and determined. She decided to start a cooking business in her home and asked me to help her develop the plan.

As I gathered more information about Marsha's life, it became clear that she was too overwhelmed to make this kind of change so quickly. I explained that making important decisions (which would impact her family) while under stress was a recipe for trouble. Before she could even think about a new business, Marsha first needed to free up her time and energy.

More often than not, clients simply need permission to take good care of themselves. During our initial coaching session, I suggested to Marsha that we focus on her self-care and look for small changes she could make to give herself more time and energy. I asked her to hire a housekeeper to handle the cleaning and laundry, and I gave her the names of several to call. Providing this resource made it easier for Marsha to take action quickly before any reservation set in. I also recommended that she find a babysitter to give her at least one night during the week to herself. She arranged to exchange babysitting evenings with a friend in the neighborhood.

Although these seemed like small changes, they had big results. Marsha could now relax more in the evenings and enjoy time with her children on the weekends. With the added time and space in her schedule, her life began to feel more balanced, and from a more centered place she could rethink her plans. Marsha agreed that diving into a new business was a mistake. Instead, she spent the next six months eliminating the energy drains in her life, trimming her spending habits to save extra money, and talking with friends about her business goals. Over time, these friends started sending her clients one by one. Marsha was then able to make a transition from a full-time job to part-time work as she continued to build her new business in an orderly fashion. One year later, Marsha had a good, solid client base and was able to quit her job without any interruption in income.

Creating a life that you love takes courage, commitment, and hard work. Most clients are surprised when I ask them to focus on their lives instead of their careers or personal goals. I've learned that shaping up one's life is the key to success. It's my job to help clients overcome the blocks to a high-quality life by staying focused on the steps that will get them from where they are to where they want to be.

My initial work with clients is focused on self-care—freeing up their time and identifying and eliminating what drains their energy. The idea of adding more work by encouraging them to set goals or take on anything new makes no sense when they've already got a full plate (and most of them do). Instead, I focus on clearing the plates to immediately improve the quality of their lives.

Sometimes it feels impossible to focus on your life when a demanding job is taking up all your time and energy. This is when it's important to remember that you are in charge of your life. With the right tools, you can make even the most challenging situation work for you. Let's revisit Shirley's situation to further explain my point.

Shirley manages seventy-five employees in her sales division. She is responsible for increasing revenues by 25 percent before the end of the year. Feeling stressed out and overworked, Shirley was concerned with taking care of her health while trying to meet this goal.

As I became familiar with Shirley's typical workday, I could see why she was on overload. Her voice mail filled on a daily basis, and she was overwhelmed with unreturned phone calls. She often arrived late for meetings (and sometimes missed them completely). And she drank coffee by the gallon. Not only was this busyness taking its toll on Shirley—it was frustrating her staff as well.

Once I had a good idea of what was going on, I told Shirley the truth as I saw it—she needed to get some support and start taking consistent time off for herself. I explained to her that without a strong foundation for her life, any business success she achieved in increased sales would be short lived.

The first step was to give Shirley permission to put herself first. She needed to let go of control and start delegating. Each week, we reviewed her voice mail message list and developed strategies for her administrative assistant to handle most of the calls. As Shirley's willingness to relinquish control increased, she gradually handed over responsibility to her assistant. Within two months, her assistant was retrieving and handling 90 percent of her calls. In the beginning, Shirley would never have thought it possible to delegate this type of task. But with permission and a plan that worked, what was once impossible was not only possible but much more effective.

Shirley also made a commitment to leave the office at 5:30 instead of the usual 8 or 8:30 P.M. This allowed her to spend the evenings with her husband and have time in her garden, something that always helped her to relax. At first, Shirley was concerned that this would be setting the wrong example to her staff, but the opposite occurred. Shirley was able to get her work done in less time. Her commitment to leave at 5:30 made her more focused and productive during the day, and she was able to be much more present for her staff, giving them the quality of direction they needed to do their jobs well.

I also encouraged Shirley to schedule fewer meetings and arrive on time to rebuild the trust she had broken with her staff. By the end of six months, Shirley felt that her life was much more balanced, and her division had increased sales by 15 percent. These are the kinds of decisions and actions that create true success.

## I'LL BE YOUR COACH

With this book I'd like to coach you to create a life that you love. At first I'll ask you to make the quality of your life the main focus of your attention. I'll support you while you learn to trust your own best instincts—your Wise Self. And I'll teach you the seven strategies to overcome the obstacles that prevent you from living the life you want. As you work through the program in this book, you'll learn to:

1. **Put yourself at the top of the list.** You'll learn to make the practice of extreme self-care your new standard for living. I'll show you how to build a strong relationship with yourself and connect with your inner wisdom to create a life that reflects your true desires.

2. **Get your priorities straight.** I'll show you how to stop reacting to life and start taking control of what gets your time and attention. You'll set new priorities that mirror what's really important to you and learn strategies to ensure that they are honored.

3. **What's draining you?** I'll show you how to identify and eliminate what drains you. Whether it's a disorganized office, a cluttered home, or the friend that constantly complains and drains your energy, I'll show you how to plug those energy drains once and for all.

4. **Invest in your financial health.** You'll learn specific ways to get your financial house in order and build financial reserves so that you no longer feel like a victim to life. And you'll attract more money by practicing these basic money management skills.

5. **What's fueling you?** I'll show you how to kick the adrenaline habit and use healthier forms of energy—like the company of good friends, fun exercise, and soul-nurturing activities.

6. **Build a "soulful" community.** I'll suggest specific ways

to surround yourself with a community of high-quality relationships that will support, challenge, and encourage you to be your best.

7. **Honor your spiritual well-being.** I'll show you how to take time for the most important relationship of all—the connection to your inner wisdom, the voice of your soul. You'll create a personal practice and spend time every day nurturing your spiritual well-being.

As you incorporate these seven strategies into your life, you'll feel better. You'll find that you're more connected to yourself and others and have a greater sense of what's really important. And then, a funny thing happens. You actually begin to *attract* better things toward you. Like my client Nicole, you send a different message into the world, and what you get back is sometimes beyond what you could have imagined.

Nicole sounded discouraged when we first spoke. She said she felt frustrated with the direction of her life and wanted a miracle— Nicole wanted a new life. She felt lonely most of the time and isolated in her work as a graphic designer. She had lost touch with several friends and spent weekends alone working at her computer.

Nicole and I met during a time of deep questioning. With good intentions, she longed to "make a difference in the world" and wanted me to help her find the right career. Nicole was convinced that a new job helping others would help her to feel better about her life. As we talked further, I suggested that Nicole make a difference in her own life first, and trust that, as a result, a much better life would actually start to just "show up."

Over the next year Nicole focused on building a relationship with herself and getting her life in order. She bought a journal and began writing in it almost every day. She kept track of how she felt as she went through this process, wrote letters of support to herself, and made lists of things she felt grateful for.

A self-proclaimed pack rat, she went through old boxes dating back to her college years and threw out all the old junk. With my support, she handled the difficult things she'd been avoiding—like getting her finances in order, creating a nurturing home, and ending a two-year relationship that she had outgrown.

Nicole was slowly realizing that she had a choice about how to live her life and that fear had kept her from taking action. With someone on her side to guide her through the process, it became much easier to make the necessary changes that would give her the kind of life she desired.

As she started to feel better about herself, the world began to see her differently. Nicole loved children, and while volunteering her design services to a local school, she was offered a job as a creative director for a new children's educational center opening nearby. This job would allow Nicole to use her creative talents to help others and meet new friends. Nicole's health improved, she rarely felt discouraged, and she even lost ten pounds of extra weight she'd been carrying for several years.

Nicole also began to reawaken her spiritual life by writing letters to God in her journal and attending a local Unitarian church. She felt a deepening connection to a Divine power, which added a depth of meaning to her life that she had not experienced before. One year later, Nicole said she felt like a different person—a happy person living a life that she loved.

Strange as it may sound, I now encourage my clients to focus less on finding the best career, business opportunity, or relationship. Instead, by helping them to focus on basics like creating more time for themselves, learning to say no, and investing in their financial health, our work together becomes a spiritual journey. As they focus their attention on improving the quality of their life, the life they are meant to live unfolds before our eyes.

## HOW TO GET THE MOST FROM THIS BOOK

This book captures this journey in a program designed to attract *your* best life. If you'd like to improve the quality of your life, this book provides an important ingredient for your success—the guiding hand of someone who's helped others do the same. As your personal coach, I've included the same checklists, exercises, and resources that have helped my clients overcome the obstacles to better lives.

To get the most from this program, I strongly recommend the following guidelines:

- Review the entire book before doing the program.
- Once you've reviewed the book, choose a partner or create a small "coaching group" of people who want to actively support each other in creating a high-quality life. Since a book can never replace the powerful relationship shared with a coach, finding others to support you through this program is the next best thing. To do this, you'll want to use the following guidelines:

1. Choose a person (or persons) you can trust.
2. Be sure that they have the time and desire to commit to the process of completing the book.
3. Pick a regular time to meet (at least once a month). You can do this in person or over the phone.
4. Read one chapter at a time before getting together.
5. Once you're together, use the following format to make these gatherings productive and supportive:
   a. Start the meeting by sharing your success. What did you accomplish? How do you feel? Applaud each other for a job well done.
   b. Spend time discussing the chapter that you've read in preparation for this meeting. Complete any group exercises contained in the chapter.
   c. Decide on specific actions that you'll each take before your next meeting.
   d. Ask for help. Use the last fifteen minutes of the meeting to share any support that you need. What's stopping you from moving forward?

Where do you feel blocked? What do you need to take action in spite of your fear? A helping hand? An extra phone call to check in? A specific resource or referral?

- Buy yourself a journal to use in conjunction with this book.
- Each time you see the words "Take Action!" use this as a sign to take action immediately. One small step will make a big difference. As soon as you finish a chapter, start with one easy step. Success builds momentum, and before you know it, you'll find yourself excited to move onto the next step.
- Ask for help. If any part of this program feels too challenging, get the support you need to stay in action. Whether it's from your partner or your coaching group, speak up and ask for help.

    You'll also find help in the resource section at the end of each chapter. These sections contain the names of books, videos, and relevant people, as well as other information that can make it easier to take action.
- Celebrate your success. After completing an action, take time out to reward yourself.
- Take your time. The program contained in this book is not a quick fix. It's meant to be worked through over time. For most, this program could take one to three years to complete.
- Stay open-minded. Some of the stories you'll read throughout the book seem magical. They *are* magical. When you make your self-care a priority and take action toward your highest good, you ignite the magic that's available to us all. A divine force will guide you toward a high-quality life. Watch for this magic along the way—it's the best motivating force of all.

Now it's your turn. Good luck!

# 1

---

# Put Yourself

# at the Top

# of the List

---

On a cold winter morning in December 1984 I was given a gift that would change my life forever. Early in the morning, around six, I was aroused from a deep sleep by a phone ringing in the distance. As I put the phone to my ear, I heard my mother sobbing and saying something about a fire. I bolted upright in bed, banging my head against the wall, and quickly tried to get my bearings. "Mom!" I yelled. "What's wrong?" No sound—just more crying. "Mom," I continued in as calm a voice as I could muster, "take a deep breath, calm down, and tell me what's wrong." She started to catch her breath and, between sobs, said four words I'll never forget: "family business" and "in flames."

I jumped out of bed, threw on some clothes, and raced to my car. I still remember scraping an icy spot off my windshield *while* driving to the scene. Once there, I couldn't believe my eyes. Our office building, the tallest historical building left in town, was heavily engulfed by thick black smoke that parted only for an occasional flash of flames. The building looked like a raging inferno. For a moment I stood staring at the fire in total disbelief, trying to take in the reality of the scene. Then I remembered my dad.

Scrambling to make my way through the crowd, I searched desperately for my father. It's funny how, during a crisis, certain images freeze in your mind forever. I can still remember seeing him perched on the steps of a building across the street, self-consciously wiping tears from his face as I ran toward him.

Together, in a state of shock, we watched as firefighters tried to recover pieces of anything that could be saved. My office, located on the street level at the front of the building, had been framed by a wall of windows that allowed me to sit at my desk and look out over the street. Now I was looking in, watching my artwork, furniture, and equipment quickly vanish in the flames. I was completely powerless to help as my whole life disappeared before my eyes.

Watching the fruits of my hard work dissolve so early in my career taught me some important lessons. In an instant, life as you know it can disappear forever. All the things that were so important just one minute before—like the big project that must be completed by 5 P.M. or the deal you're trying to close—are rendered meaningless in a matter of seconds. Instead, you immediately turn your thoughts to the people in your life.

I saw firsthand how fragile life is and how important it is to pay attention to how we spend our time on earth. I suppose a fire is like any natural disaster—it puts you in touch with how quickly life can change and how valuable every moment really is.

As the days passed, we began to assess the physical damage. Sifting through the rubble that was once my office, I found myself crying over the silliest things. My telephone, the lifeline of my business, had melted, leaving behind a small puddle of black plastic. The little metal replica of a postal mailbox, a favorite conversation piece that I kept on my desk to collect spare change, was reduced to a pool of blue gunk. And my adding machine, the extension of my right arm, had completely disappeared.

Although these things seemed incidental to others, they were very symbolic to me. I had become attached to them in the same way that others become attached to favorite mementos they've collected to display around their homes. Sad to say, my office had become my home.

This tragedy forced me to take a close look at how I was living my life. Despite external success (or what passed for success in the small town where I grew up), I wasn't happy. Work was stressful, and the hours were long and hard. My life felt like one long workday after another with very little else in between. I was so consumed with getting the work done, pleasing my clients, and keeping the boss happy that I never lifted my head up from my desk long enough to see what it was doing to my life. Now I was starting to notice.

All my time and energy was being spent on the needs of others at the expense of my own needs. Work had become my life, and things were severely out of balance. The burning building became a metaphor—I was burning up the precious time that I had on this planet. I needed to slow down, take an honest look at my life, and start asking myself what *I* wanted. I needed to get my priorities straight.

Many people experience personal crises. It may be the sudden death of a family member, a flood or fire that ruins your home and possessions, or the diagnosis of a life-threatening illness. Once you've been through it, you're never the same. It changes you on a very deep level. One of the gifts that surviving a personal crisis gives you is the motivation to reevaluate your life and take note of what really matters. Your perception changes, and you find yourself asking some important questions. Am I really happy? Where do I feel truly satisfied? What do I want out of life, and what changes do I need to make to get it?

Not everyone needs a personal crisis to rethink how they live their lives. For some, the wake-up call comes in the form of a persistent inner voice that reminds them that something is missing. Maybe you simply see someone sitting on a park bench enjoying an ice cream cone and you long for the freedom and time to do that. Or you hear yourself talk over and over again about the flower garden you'd like to plant or the class you'd like to take, yet you notice that you never seem to do these things you want to do.


## YOUR LIFE IS NOT YOUR WORK

During a personal crisis or after listening to your persistent inner voice long enough, your work life gets reevaluated as well. Do I get enough satisfaction for all that I put into my work? What's the return on my investment of time and energy? How much time am I spending on the job? You begin to realize that there is much more to life than your career or your business.

Years of conditioning have taught us to look toward work for the meaning and fulfillment we desire. This is evidenced by those who call asking me for help in finding or building a career that will fulfill their "life purpose." Or the business owners who are anxious to get the right "mission statement" completed so they can be on their way to living the life they're "meant to live." Expecting your work to provide you with this kind of profound meaning and fulfillment is a setup. You end up investing too much of your time and energy in work, desperately searching for something that cannot be found there—a life.

As a work-centered culture, we've lost touch with ourselves. We skip lunch or eat on the run, conduct business while driving our cars, and rush to pick up the kids at the end of a long day. We barely have time for ourselves, let alone quality time with those we love. Cecile Andrews, in her book *The Circle of Simplicity,* makes some startling points. She writes, "Couples spend an average of 12 minutes a day talking to each other" and "40 minutes per week playing with children." And it's no wonder we're exhausted—she goes on to say that "half of all Americans don't get enough sleep."

We spend well beyond forty hours a week at our jobs, commuting long distances, and, with the dramatic increase in home-based businesses, many of us never leave work at all anymore. The average number of hours spent per week on work (commuting, actual work time, weekend worry, and preparation) by the clients who come to me for support ranges from fifty-five to eighty hours. Such a lifestyle takes its toll. My clients are exhausted from climbing the corporate ladder, dressing for success, and trying to maintain the balancing act of work and family. They're tired of work that requires them to check their values and self-care at the door in exchange for position and salary. And they're fed up with working long hours and never feeling caught up, appreciated, or satisfied.

Vacations have become recuperation periods instead of time for leisure and recreation. And those few weeks a year are never enough. In 1992, Joe Dominguez and Vicki Robin noted in *Your Money or Your Life* that "the average North American works 20 percent more today than in 1973 and has 32 percent less free time per week." And if the lives of my clients are any indication, the percentage of time spent working is still on the rise, leaving free time relegated to a few short hours per week.

With the increase in stress-related illnesses like heart disease, chronic fatigue, and cancer—the kind of reality that often brings people face-to-face with how a work-centered way of life isn't working—you'd think that more people would be jumping off the fast track. But they're not. Why is it so difficult to start putting our own needs first?

For some, a work-centered life feels necessary to make ends meet. Parents, wanting to give their children a good education, work hard to earn the money that will allow them to send their kids to the best schools. Single women, wanting to live in safe neighborhoods, pay for it with higher rents. And the continuation of downsizing still leaves many employees concerned that if they don't work long and hard, they'll be replaced by the competition who stands ready to take their place.

Others, still caught up in the "myth of more," continue to search for happiness through the pursuit of more money, better jobs, nicer things, and fancier vacations. But working hard to acquire more is not paying off. By now, most of us have realized that "having it all" is not what it's cracked up to be. A job that pays an impressive salary and provides a prestigious position does not bring happiness. Instead, it brings lots of responsibility and high levels of stress, which leave you feeling empty and out of touch with what's really important.

George Leonard, a pioneer in the field of human potential and author of several books (including *Mastery* and *The Life We Are Given),* in his address to the Association for Humanistic Psychology in 1989 stated that "48 percent of 4,126 male executives saw their lives as empty and meaningless despite years of professional striving." This emptiness is often marked by an underlying sadness that, according to one client, "rises to the surface when I slow down long enough to feel it." A forty-seven-year-old doctor who after four years finally spent a week by himself doing nothing said, "I was surprised at how much I just wanted to sit around and cry. I don't know why, but I felt an incredible amount of sorrow for the loss of myself and the life that was passing me by." Another client admits that a "nagging sense of loneliness" follows her around in spite of the number of people involved in her life.

Such feelings can be the reason why some people stay so busy. Slowing down means unleashing the pent-up emotions that have built up over time. But feelings of loneliness and sadness are normal when you give yourself room to feel. It can be a frightening experience to stop and take a truthful look at how life is passing you by.

Sometimes the problem has to do with feeling pulled in too many directions. With all the demands of their time, clients who lead busy lives find it easy to forget about themselves. In my earlier years in the tax business, I never stopped long enough to notice how crazy my life had become. I was too busy taking care of the needs of my clients, my staff, and my boss to realize that I had needs too!

When you're exhausted at the end of the day, you simply do not have energy to spend on yourself. As my client Bea, a mother of two who works full-time, said, "Forget about me, I don't have the energy for *my* life. Sure I miss my friends, but at the end of the day, I'm so tired that the last thing I want to do is talk on the phone. When friends call to chat I resent it. And going to the gym? When? I wake up, pack my kids off to school, and run out the door to go to the office. When I get home at seven I'm exhausted, the kids need to be fed, and my husband wants to talk about his day. By ten I'm passed out on the couch, and the next day it just starts all over again."

Another reason why clients continue to work crazy hours is that they don't know what else to do with their time. My client Janice realized this during one of our coaching sessions early in our work together. Janice was a vivacious, outgoing public relations specialist. Her days were spent meeting with clients, courting media contacts, and planning new campaigns. Janice was always the center of attention and excelled at everything she did. At the age of forty-one, she seemed to be on top of the world. She traveled internationally, stayed at the finest hotels, and had a list of clients wanting to work with her. But Janice had a different perspective of her life.

In the privacy of our coaching calls, Janice confessed that her "public face" was simply a mask she put on every morning before going to work. Underneath this mask was a frightened young woman. Successful on the outside, on the inside Janice felt like a fraud. In spite of her successful track record, Janice was slowly losing steam. She secretly wondered how much longer she would be able to continue at her fast-track pace before getting sick. Janice worked most evenings, rarely got a good night's sleep, and found herself overreacting to the slightest mistakes made by her staff. She said she felt "dead" inside, as though "one morning I woke up and my enthusiasm for life had disappeared."

When I asked her to reflect on how she could start to make her self-care a priority, she replied, "The truth is, when I ask myself what I'd do if I wasn't working, it scares me to death to realize that I don't have an answer." Once Janice heard herself say the truth out loud, she stepped out of denial and into a place where our real work could begin. She was ready to put herself first.

Does your life feel like one long workday after another? Let me remind you that the most important part of your life is you. You are the sum of your parts, only one of which is work. Whether you're headed for burnout like Janice or feel like you're already there, decide now to make your self-care a priority by putting yourself at the top of your "to do" list!

## EXTREME SELF-CARE

As your coach, I'd like to begin our work together by giving you permission to make the quality of your life your top priority. A high-quality life starts with a high-quality you. My basic coaching philosophy in working with clients is one of extreme self-care—the foundation of a rich and fulfilling life. This means putting your self-care above anything else—saying no unless it's an absolute yes, choosing to spend your time and energy on things that bring you joy, and making decisions based on what *you* want instead of what others want. It's a challenging concept for most.

Making your self-care a priority can be scary, even offensive, at first. Yet, as you begin to filter your decisions through the lens of extreme self-care, you'll find that your nagging inner voice becomes a strong ally in helping you to make better choices. You'll leave work early to keep that dinner engagement with a friend, or you'll go out for a walk during lunch instead of working straight through. And, best of all, you'll discover that when you start practicing extreme self-care, a Divine force rallies behind you to support your decisions and will actually make your life easier. The simple "coincidence" that occurred for my client Melissa demonstrates my point.

Melissa was a consultant who taught managers how to communicate more effectively with their employees. She had a very demanding client who constantly called her after hours in crisis. Melissa was fed up with the intrusion on her time and wanted me to help her set better boundaries.

When I asked her to assess the situation and tell me what she needed to do to honor her extreme self-care, she thought a moment and reluctantly admitted that it was probably time to let this client go. Melissa knew that to truly honor herself this would be the best choice, but she was afraid to do it. This client was very pushy, and Melissa didn't know how to complete the relationship in a way that would be respectful yet firm.

We discussed her options, and I helped her plan what she would say to end the relationship gracefully. When Melissa called the client, she was surprised to learn that he had given his notice and would soon be leaving the company. Relieved, she expressed her good wishes and agreed to meet with him to finalize their work.

These are the kinds of synchronistic events that can occur when you are committed to taking extremely good care of yourself. I used to think they were only coincidences, but now, having seen it happen time and again with clients, I'm convinced that a higher order takes over to support us when we make the choice to honor ourselves in spite of our fear or discomfort.

Extreme self-care begins with learning to be selfish. For some, the word "selfish" conjures up negative reactions, and yet there is a very positive side to it as well. For example, we've all been told by flight attendants that when flying on an airplane with children, we should put the oxygen mask on ourselves *first* in the event of an emergency. By doing this we can then care for our child. When you practice extreme self-care and put yourself first, you are then fully available to others without resentment or anger.

Initially, you may feel some resistance to being selfish. You might feel guilty, uncomfortable, uncaring, unspiritual, or concerned about the reaction of others. But tell your friends and family that you've decided to take care of your "Self." They may very well react (as a matter of fact, you can expect that some people in your life will give you a hard time), but remember, *your life is at stake.* You deserve to take care of your Self.

When a coworker teases you about leaving at 5 P.M., or your spouse feels threatened when you want time to yourself, or your children get angry when they don't have your attention when they want it, you can remind them that this is part of your extreme self-care. Let them know that you'll end up becoming a better father, mother, husband, wife, friend, and that ultimately everyone will win. Over time, you'll realize that honoring yourself is the greatest gift you can give to someone else.

Since coaching is about taking action, let's begin with specific actions you can take to practice extreme self-care. In the following pages, I've outlined a plan to help you get started. Take at least one action every day. Forget about perfection. The object is to set in motion a higher order for your life.

As you start to free up more of your time (chapter 2) and restore your energy (chapter 3), you'll be able to spend even more time on your self-care. For now, while your plate is full, take it slow and easy.

### Getting to Know You

One of the most important aspects of extreme self-care begins with reestablishing a relationship with yourself—becoming familiar with your needs and desires; essentially, getting to know *you*. Since most of us spend far too much time on the needs of others, we lose touch with the most important relationship of all—the relationship to ourselves. How do we reestablish this relationship?

### Take Action! Start a Journal

The first thing I'd like you to do is get yourself a journal. Set aside some time to find one that *feels* like you. Don't just pick up any old notebook—find the right size, shape, color, texture, and design that works for you. Do you prefer lined or unlined? Big or small? Pick one that gives you plenty of room to write and one that will be easy to carry with you.

Throughout this book, I'll ask you to use this journal for various exercises and self-reflection. Keeping a journal is a great way to start an ongoing dialogue with yourself. At the age of thirteen I started my first journal to help me deal with the challenges of adolescence. I found comfort in writing my thoughts and feelings in a safe place I could call my own. It has remained such an important outlet for me that I'm always surprised at people's hesitation to begin the practice of journaling.

For those who are hesitant, the problem is often twofold: perfectionism and lack of time. Perfectionism takes the joy and adventure out of journal writing. Our internal editor or critic kicks in, and the practice becomes painful instead of self-reflective and nurturing. It's normal when starting a journal to hear the voice of your inner critic telling you what you should and shouldn't write. I've found two helpful things to avoid being influenced by this voice.

First, write continuously, without stopping. Put the focus on filling the page, not writing the perfect text. Don't get caught up in perfection—you'll lose the experience. Make mistakes. Don't bother crossing your *t*'s or dotting your *i*'s—just keep writing. By writing nonstop, you'll soon uncover thoughts and feelings you may have been unaware of—that's how journal writing becomes an adventure.

If that doesn't work, let your inner critic write for a while. Start writing what you hear in your head. Let your critic run free with its dialogue of "This is a waste of time" or "That last line was stupid" or "You're not doing it right." Pretty soon you'll find that the inner critic gets tired and you're able to go back to your original writing. Before you know it, your journal will become a trusted companion.

If your life is busy and full of commitments, don't expect to write long passages every day. Give yourself a break. Until we start clearing your plate, allow yourself to write a paragraph or two when you have a spare, quiet moment. Remember, we're going for progress, not perfection.

If you live with others, let them know that your journal is private and for your eyes only. If there is any question about whether your privacy will be honored, I recommend that you find a safe place to hide or secure your journal. This way, you won't be tempted to censor your writing.

Later on, journal writing will give you a wonderful chance to look back over your life and see how you've grown. Journals become filled with the richness of your life experience—the pain and pleasure, the significant events, the questioning and search for meaning, all that influences who you are. Many times I've gone back over old journals and smiled at the person I was becoming. It's a wonderful ritual for birthdays or special times when you want to reconnect with your past and acknowledge the changes you've made.

To get your journal started, choose one of the sentences below and spend some time writing.

- The ten things I am most grateful for are . . .
- What I love most about myself is . . .
- The idea of keeping a journal feels . . .
- My most secret desire is . . .
- I'm most afraid of . . .
- The changes that would move me forward in my life are . . .

As you get used to journal writing, you'll find it becomes a welcomed habit. Two journal exercises will help you to get to know yourself even better, but before you embark on those, let's carve out some time in your busy schedule for your new priority of extreme self-care.

### Take Action! Choose Your Sacred "Date Night"

When you meet someone for a date and decide that you'd like to explore the relationship further, what do you do? You spend more time together. You find time in your busy schedules to meet, and when you do, you talk for hours, asking endless questions and sharing personal stories and experiences. It's funny how we always seem to find the time to spend with others and not with ourselves. But this is exactly what you'll need to do to reconnect with yourself. I'd like you to set aside time each week to devote to your relationship with yourself—a sacred date night.

When I suggested that Janice, my client who was facing burnout, find a time in her busy schedule just for herself, she decided that Sunday nights would become sacred. She set aside this time to spend alone reevaluating her life and taking good care of herself. Sometimes she simply turned off the phone and spent time journaling, cooking her favorite meal, or relaxing in a hot bath. Other times she went to a movie alone or to her favorite restaurant for dinner.

Sunday nights became her sacred date night, and she didn't let anyone interrupt them. At first Janice was met with some resistance from friends wanting to see her, but, as I mentioned before, by letting them know up front that her self-care was now a priority, they quickly got the message. In fact, a couple of her friends actually began doing the same thing.

What time will you set aside for yourself? Choose a time during each week that you'll be able to hold sacred, and write that time here:

_____

Next, think about some of the things that you'd most like to do to take good care of yourself. List the first three that come to mind:

1. _____
2. _____
3. _____

Now that you've set aside the time for yourself, the following two writing exercises will help you gain an objective view of where you are in your life.

### Take Action! Write Your Life Story

First, I'd like you to use your journal to capture the story of your life. This is a powerful exercise in honoring who you are and where you've come from. I always begin my coaching relationships with this exercise not only to get to know my clients better but to help them get to know themselves. Writing about the details and history that have made you who you are today will help you to understand and appreciate the choices you've made that have brought you to this point in your life.

What events most affected you? Why? When did you feel loved, cherished, angry, betrayed, fully seen and heard? Which events will you never forget? What made you stop dead in your tracks and head in another direction? Do certain types of people keep showing up in your life? The answers to these questions weave together the fabric called you and can provide you valuable insight.

Sometimes writing your life story can shine light on a present-day challenge. For example, when I first asked Florence, a forty-eight-year-old bank manager, to write her life story, she felt overwhelmed by the request. I suggested that she make it easy by creating a simple outline that chronicled the significant events in her life and the people who were involved.

As Florence wrote about these events, she was surprised to see a pattern emerge. She had a history of being involved in relationships with cold and controlling women. This pattern had started with her mother and continued throughout her life, leaving Florence feeling confused and unable to trust strong women.

One of Florence's original reasons for requesting my help was to deal with a difficult coworker, her assistant manager. Florence said that her assistant seemed introverted and unfriendly. She never said much in meetings, and this made Florence nervous because she never knew where she stood with this woman.

Florence confided in me that she felt "defensive around her, almost bracing myself for a fight." After reviewing her life story, she understood why the relationship with her assistant felt so strained. This coworker was the kind of woman who kept to herself and just got her job done. Florence experienced this as cold and controlling. But once she saw the pattern in her life story, she had a different perspective and was able to stop taking her assistant's behavior so personally.

As soon as Florence realized that her defensiveness was in response to women from her past, she approached her coworker differently. I suggested that she invite this woman to lunch with the intention of establishing a better relationship. Florence was pleasantly surprised to find that her coworker appreciated the invitation and said she looked forward to getting to know her better.

What will you discover while writing the story of your life? If the idea feels overwhelming, don't let that stop you. Be creative. Write the significant events of your life in bullet-list form. Break the action into smaller steps. Devote a half-hour on your weekly date night to writing an ongoing story of your life.

To begin, separate your life into decades. As you review each decade in your mind, complete these sentences:

> *The significant events during this part of my life were . . .*
> *The one event I remember most is . . .*
> *These events affected my life in the following ways:*
> *The person(s) who influenced me most was (were) . . .*
> *This part of my life affects me now in the following way:*

Don't be surprised if you find it difficult to remember past events—most people do. Ask friends and family for help, look at photo albums, or watch old home movies and let them trigger your memories. Not only will writing your life story give you valuable information about you, the actual process itself will deepen the connection you have with yourself.

Most people I've worked with who have completed their life stories usually feel a strong sense of self-love and compassion for all they've been through. This is a key way to strengthen the relationship with yourself. You'll learn a lot about what motivates you, and you may even identify patterns of behavior that could get in the way of making some of the changes outlined in this book. For example, you may notice that throughout your life you've had a difficult time setting boundaries with others and therefore may have trouble taking care of your own needs. Or you may notice a pattern of procrastination that's prevented you from completing projects with ease. Knowing this will help prepare you for the ways you'll need to grow to create the life you most want.

Review this exercise with your coaching partner or group. When you complete your life stories, share them with each other and have your partner or group ask the following questions:

- What did you learn about yourself from this exercise?
- What patterns or themes have you identified? Are you afraid to make changes? Do you settle for less? Do certain people or certain kinds of people keep showing up in your life? Are you a risk taker? Did your interest in certain areas start early?
- Who has influenced you the most? Has their influence supported you or hindered you?
- If you could change a part of your past, which part would it be? Why?
- Do you notice anything from your past that may stop you from making changes in the present or future?
- What are you most proud of?

Write the answers to these questions in your journal. As you discuss your life story with others, you may be surprised to notice similarities you share with them. One thing I've learned from reading plenty of life stories is how alike we all are. The events and details may be different, but the underlying lessons and desires are all very similar.

### Take Action! Expand Your Vision to Include Your "Whole" Life

Next, I'd like you to take a closer look at how you're living your life now. One way to move beyond a work-centered life is to become aware of the other areas you may be neglecting.

Life is made up of many facets, and no one facet is more or less important than another. A meaningful life is one of balance. I'd like to give you permission to expand your view of life beyond work to other areas—your emotional and physical health, your relationships, your spiritual well-being, your leisure time, and the sharing of yourself with others. By putting your attention on these areas, you become more aware of what's missing in your life.

When you live a more holistic life, you naturally distribute your time and energy differently, creating a sense of balance that leaves you less vulnerable to crisis when changes occur in one area or another. That way, if you lose your job or find yourself facing a divorce, you can fall back on the other parts of your life to support you. A problem in one area does not have to feel like a life-threatening crisis, as it did for my client Mark.

Mark had been in a relationship with a woman he had met while sailing during a summer vacation three years earlier. Their relationship was driving him crazy. He and his girlfriend fought constantly about everything from money to the differences in their friends. Over the last year, Mark had tried to end the relationship several times, deciding that their basic differences would make it impossible to stay together. But Mark said his life felt empty as soon as he was on his own, and the pain of his loneliness would prompt him to go back and try again.

On a gut level, Mark knew that the relationship needed to end, but he couldn't bring himself to do it. When his girlfriend wasn't around, he said he felt unable to function, as if a giant void was left in his life. Unfortunately, Mark couldn't function when she was around, either. The problems in their relationship made him feel anxious most of the time. Between the stress of fighting and breaking up, he couldn't concentrate on work or other activities. Instead, he spent most of his time obsessing about his girlfriend and worrying about what life would be like on his own.

When I explained to Mark that his whole life revolved around this relationship and therefore made ending it feel like the end of his life, he began to view the problem differently. Between being with his girlfriend, recuperating from their fights, and worrying about living on his own, nearly 80 percent of his time and energy was being focused on this area of his life at the expense of other areas. It was no surprise that Mark was afraid to lose this relationship—without it, he didn't have much life left.

With my help, Mark decided to focus on a more balanced way of living. He didn't end the relationship right away. Instead, he limited the time he spent with his girlfriend and started to reconnect with his friends. He went back to his local gym and started working out and, at the suggestion of a close friend, found a therapist to help him untangle his mixed feelings. Three months later, Mark ended the relationship for good and began the process of grieving and moving on. By spreading his time, energy, and attention to other areas of his life, he felt much more empowered and able to be on his own.

Where might your life be out of balance? What gets the majority of your time and attention? Are there areas that you've been neglecting or putting on hold? If you're like most people, you wish you had more time to dedicate to your health, to have fun, or to spend with loved ones. The diagrams opposite illustrate the difference between a holistic life and the kind of life that most clients live prior to our coaching work. (If you're an "at home" mom or dad, you can substitute for the work section—and probably add to it—the care of your children and household.)

The chart on the top diagrams life from a holistic perspective—a balanced, whole life. The chart on the bottom diagrams the typical balance of a client's life before we start our work together. As you see in the "out of balance" pie chart, most people spend more time contributing to others in some way than they spend on their spiritual well-being or having fun. And the relationships portion of the "out of balance" pie chart does not necessarily represent the "good times"—it may indicate time spent on providing care for an aging parent or dealing with a troubled relationship. In any event, most clients are not living their "whole" lives.

Don't be surprised if you feel a sense of sadness as you review these diagrams. As I mentioned earlier, it's not unusual to feel a sense of loss when you stop to look at how you've been living your life, assuming it's not the way you want it to be. If work has taken up so much of your time that your health is suffering, or, if you're paying

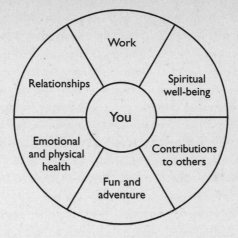

**A Balanced, "Whole" Life**

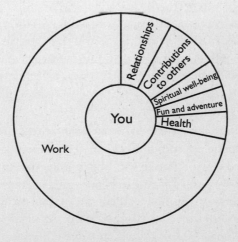

**An "Out of Balance" Life**

so much attention to a relationship that you haven't put enough of your energy into "you," then the reality of this may be difficult to face.

I know you can create your life in such a way that you are able to spend time more evenly distributed among each of these areas. With an honest assessment of what gets your attention and the willingness to take action, you can bring your life into balance. Awareness comes first; then you must take the actions needed to make a change.

My client Karen was able to get her life back by making a major change. A successful interior designer, she loved her work. It gave her an outlet for her creativity and allowed her to meet new and interesting people. There was only one problem—the company she worked for was located too far from her home. When traffic was bad, her commute time could reach three hours per day.

When Karen viewed her "whole life," she calculated that, including her daily commute, the time dedicated to work represented almost 75 percent of her life. She had very little time left for her family and friends, fun activities, her health, and her spiritual well-being.

When I encouraged Karen to look seriously at the cost of living so far from work, both practically and emotionally, she realized that she had to make a change. She loved her home but had suffered with the commute long enough. Although it was a tough decision, Karen decided to keep the job and sell the house. When she completed the relocation and moved closer to work, Karen had almost fifteen extra hours a week available for things like art classes, trips to the gym, and social time with friends.

Now let's look at your life. Take out your journal and, as you read through the following sections, notice the areas that want more attention from you. Pay attention to how you feel—a twinge of conflict, a feeling of "Yes!," or a tug at your heart are all signs that you've just read something important. Write about this awareness in your journal.

## Emotional and Physical Health

It's easy to ignore our emotional and physical health until there's a problem. Most of us wait until it's too late. We lead busy, hectic lives, putting work or the needs of others before our own self-care. We fill our bodies with fast food, tolerate high levels of stress, and run non-stop on adrenaline. Like the Energizer bunny, the body keeps going and going—then, one day, something goes wrong. We get sick, hear the diagnosis of an unexpected illness, or notice that we just can't seem to get things done the way we used to. That's when most people, like my client Jonah, finally start paying attention to their health.

Jonah is a busy real estate broker who maintained the title of top salesperson in his office for three years. Proud of his accomplishment, he was convinced that his success was a result of being available to customers seven days a week, twenty-four hours a day. After all, when the customer wanted to buy or sell, the realtor had to be there.

The stress of interruptions during family dinners, buyers suddenly changing their minds, and sellers expecting quick sales eventually caught up with him. His wife complained that she never saw him, he frequently missed his children's school events, and eventually his physical health began to suffer. Jonah didn't have the energy he used to have and found himself getting winded and tired more easily. When he finally saw his doctor, Jonah was told that his blood pressure was too high and that he was suffering from fatigue. If he didn't slow down, his doctor ordered, he was headed for serious trouble.

Jonah was forced to reevaluate his priorities. Was being number one really that important? Did he have time to enjoy the money that he worked so hard to make? How would his poor health affect his family life? Jonah decided to make a change. He agreed to take one day off each weekend and schedule showings only on two nights during the week. He hired a local college student to help with administrative tasks and began the search for a licensed assistant who could eventually replace him when he was unavailable. In the beginning, Jonah lost customers, but he gained something far more important—he got his life back.

We've all heard the saying "Without your health you have nothing." The thing that can interrupt our lives in an instant is the very thing we often give the least amount of attention to. Living with too much stress causes us to engage in the very habits we try to avoid: We overeat when we're upset, skip exercise when we're too busy, or use caffeine to keep us going throughout the day. Eventually we get sick and are forced to stop and care for our health so we can get back in the race once again. It becomes a vicious cycle.

Caring for your body is much more than curing an illness. Good health means having plenty of energy to do all that you want to do. The results of how we live our lives are reflected in our bodies. When we get sick, it indicates that we've already been under a great deal of stress. How many times have you been sick with a cold or the flu and suddenly realized how much you take your health for granted? As you free up your time (chapter 2) and restore your energy (chapter 3), you'll find that taking good care of your body will get easier. You can make your health a priority before illness strikes. Until then, is there one simple change you can make now to improve your physical health? Write that change in your journal.

What about your emotional health? Current mind/body medical research shows that our emotions have a major impact on our physical health. Doctors are finally acknowledging the link between our mind and body and that illness may be influenced by our emotional state. When you feel emotionally secure, you're able to be much more proactive and much less reactive in your life. This allows you to make smart choices, and smart choices make for good health.

Caring for your emotional health may mean using the support of a therapist, making time for solitude and quiet contemplation, or having a good laugh with friends. Knowing what makes you feel good and building that into your daily schedule will raise your spirits, keep your attitude upbeat, and protect your overall health.

What supports your emotional health? A long talk with a close friend? The inspiration of a good book? When my client Lorraine wanted a way to reduce the stress that she felt from working as an emergency room nurse, she decided to make it a fun project.

When I asked Lorraine to think of a time when she felt most relaxed, she mentioned a summer cottage that she and her husband had rented five years earlier. As I listened to her talk about this vacation, I noticed that the things that made her most happy had to do with what she saw. Lorraine described a place filled with beauty both inside and out. From the fine art displayed on the walls, the rooms painted with pastel colors that made her feel calm and relaxed, to the ocean view from the bedroom window, Lorraine felt nurtured by the beauty that surrounded her.

With the discovery that beauty was an important ingredient for her emotional health, I asked Lorraine to create a space in her home that looked and felt just as relaxing. She chose to transform the den, and with her husband's support she painted the walls with her favorite soft colors and filled it with artwork that touched her deeply. Each day when she came home from work, she spent time relaxing and enjoying this new oasis of peace and tranquility.

Think about a time when you felt peaceful and relaxed. Where were you? What were you doing? Write these thoughts in your journal.

## Relationships

The relationships you share with loved ones are the most important ingredient of a high-quality life. They shape who you are and add meaning to your life. As human beings, we all have a need to belong, and being part of a strong community fulfills this need. When your schedule gets full, it's too easy to take for granted the people closest to you—you assume they will understand. But everyone has their limits, and putting a relationship on hold while you're busy doing something else, especially doing it time and time again, takes its toll and can eventually damage the relationship. It's never too late to rebuild an important relationship.

My client David thought that he needed to add more fun to his life. A busy executive, David had been married for fifteen years and had one child. He and his wife, a successful lawyer, worked full-time and barely saw each other. With David's busy travel schedule, they practically lived separate lives.

Now and then, David felt restless and thought that he was getting bored with the routine of his work—hence his desire to add more fun to his life. But when I asked him to take time out each week for himself, he discovered that his restlessness was a cover-up for the loss and sadness he felt at not having a loving, available partner to share his life with. In the past, when he connected with this pain, he would plunge himself back into his world of work and travel.

During our coaching sessions, I reminded David of what a strong, fulfilling partnership could add to his life—someone to love and be loved by, a deep sexual connection, a partner to share fun and adventurous times with, and the wonderful feeling that someone was always on his side. Not only was David missing this in his marriage, but he lived in a constant state of conflict by not addressing it with his wife.

When a relationship is strong, it enriches your life and provides you with a sense of security. When it's weak, it wears you down and drains your energy, whether you consciously realize it or not. David acknowledged how much emotional energy his "roommate relationship" was costing him and decided to approach his wife about getting some help.

Are there relationships that you've been taking for granted that need your time and attention? Friends you haven't seen in a while? Have you spent enough time with your family lately? Don't wait for trouble to set in. As you review the following list, ask yourself whether you have a relationship that could use some additional care. Write the names of these people in your journal.

| | |
|---|---|
| *Spouse/Lover* | *Extended family* |
| *Friends* | *Coworkers* |
| *Parents* | *Neighbors* |
| *Children* | *Long-distance relationships* |

## Spiritual Well-Being

"Spiritual well-being" means different things to different people. For some, developing a spiritual life works within a religious context. They go to a specific house of worship, study religious texts, and take an active role in their spiritual community. For others, finding a sense of peace and centeredness that comes from spending time in nature, meditation, or studying different spiritual practices brings spiritual well-being. Today most people want to feel connected to a Divine presence in some way. However you choose to honor your spiritual well-being, you'll find true inner security and you'll open yourself up to the experience of oneness that connects us all.

My client Terry had abandoned his Catholic upbringing long ago, but the death of a close friend had stirred up questions about life after death. He found himself visiting the church of his childhood and rethinking his spiritual beliefs. During this time of questioning, Terry was introduced to Buddhism by an old high school friend during a class reunion. As he came to learn about the mindful practice of meditation, he felt a resonance with the simplicity of its message and began incorporating it into his life.

What shape is your spiritual life in? How is it different from your earlier years? What does "spiritual well-being" mean to you? Write about it in your journal.


## Fun and Adventure

Most of us experience very little fun or adventure in our lives. We save it for vacations or special holidays. But fun is a necessary part of a whole life and has a positive, powerful impact on your health and well-being. Building fun and adventure into your life on a regular basis will help you to take life less seriously and, best of all, will create the kind of memories that last a lifetime. I remember a good friend's story about simply needing to be reminded that spending money on fun was an "OK" expense.

Noreen had always dreamed of going to Tahiti. For years, she talked about it with friends, read several books about the area, and pored over travel brochures. She had the money and could easily take the time from her business, but she never scheduled the trip. One day, a good friend asked her why. Noreen thought about it and said that it didn't feel like a "legitimate expense."

When Noreen's friend told her that her strong desire and ability to go seemed to make it legitimate enough, Noreen thought about it from a different point of view. She had been brought up with a strong work ethic, where fun wasn't considered a valuable use of time. She was still living by this rule and decided to break it and schedule the trip.

Sometimes we simply need to be reminded that having fun is just as important as time spent working. What have you done for fun lately? What would you like to do? Write your ideas in your journal.

## Contributions to Others

When your cup is full, you naturally want to share with others. Being of service and offering your support to those in need brings you closer to others in a way that adds richness to your life. A smile from an elderly man who appreciates your time or the thanks from a young girl who looks forward to your visits reminds you of how fortunate you are and how we need each other.

Contribution comes in many forms—you can share your wealth, your knowledge, or your time. My client Frank found a great way to serve others while having lots of fun. Frank was a professional story-teller. Each week, he visited the local children's hospital to share his stories with the sick children. They gathered in the the playroom, and as the children laughed and cooed with delight, Frank felt an overwhelming sense of gratitude and love. This weekly trip always reminded him of how lucky he was and how giving was actually an act of receiving.

Remember a time when you shared your generosity with others. How did it feel? If you had an abundance of time, energy, and resources, where would you share yourself now? Write it in your journal.

———

Now that you've had a chance to reflect on some of the different areas that make up a balanced life, you can add those that feel personally important to you. Maybe you'd like to give yourself more time alone or engage in a special hobby or creative interest. Step back and look at your life from this new perspective. How would a balanced life look for you? What do you want more of, and what do you want less of? Create a vision of your whole life, and write about it in your journal. This new vision of your life may sound like a fantasy, but soon you'll find yourself making it a reality.

## Connect Your Head with Your Heart

Most of us have been trained to live from the neck up. Our culture values knowledge, quick thinking, and a good, solid education. But living in your head keeps you disconnected from how you feel—the key to honoring your self-care. When you're out of touch with your feelings, several things can happen. First, you make decisions that may not be in your best interest. You're more apt to push your priorities aside for the demands of others by doing what you think you should do instead of what you feel like doing. You'll know you're doing this when you find yourself saying yes to a request and then later wishing you had said no.

Second, your threshold for stress and anxiety increases, and you find yourself "putting up" with stuff. You take on more and more without realizing that you're on overload until it's too late. I can recognize this pattern in clients who suffer from one cold or illness after another. It's a signal of overwork and stress. The alarm doesn't go off until it's too late.

Third, you miss out on the richness that our feeling state provides. I call this the "soul connection," or your ability to really feel what you want in any given situation. Living in your head also impacts your ability to be deeply touched by experiences—when you live mostly in your head, you end up feeling numb.

You'll know that you're out of touch with how you feel when you find yourself feeling detached at situations when others are more emotional, like at weddings and funerals. Your mate, friends, or family members may tell you that you seem disconnected and emotionally unavailable. The connection between your head and your heart is essential to living well. Without it, you'll end up sleepwalking through life. To connect your head with your heart, try using the following exercises.

### Take Action! Stop—Breathe—Feel
Check in with how you feel before making any decisions. Relax, breathe, and mull it over. When our lives move too quickly, we can't feel, and our tendency is to act impulsively. When faced with a choice, stop, take a deep breath into your body, and notice how you feel. Are there any signs of tension? Where do you feel it? Is it something you really want to do? Breathing will move you into your body and help you connect your head with your heart. The body never lies and can become a powerful guide in helping you make decisions when you let it.

Give yourself time to really *feel* what you'd like to do. My friend Helen has a personal policy that works well. She always sleeps on any decisions that need to be made. Her friends and family know about this policy, and it gives her plenty of space to make up her mind. That way, she knows she's made the right decision.

Spend the next week consciously noticing how your body reacts to different experiences. For example, notice how you feel when you have a conversation with someone, watch a movie, or read the newspaper. Practice connecting your head and heart by giving yourself ample time to breathe deeply and check in. By strengthening this connection through daily practice, you'll instinctively start to know what you really want, and making decisions based on your extreme self-care will get easier.

### Take Action! Slow Down

As I mentioned earlier, it's difficult to feel anything when you're moving too quickly through life. Don't let a fast-paced society keep you living in your head. Start to consciously slow down and notice how you feel throughout the day. When eating a meal, eat slowly and bring your attention into the present. While walking to the bus, slow down and notice how you feel. Talk slower, write slower, stop rushing from one appointment to another. Bring yourself into the present moment by using the following simple exercise:

When you find yourself rushing around, stop and repeat the following statements to yourself:

> *[Your name], stop and be present.*
> *Take a deep breath (breathe).*
> *[Your name], go slow, notice what's around you (look around*
> *your environment).*
> *(Ask yourself) How do I feel right now?*

You can use this exercise throughout the day to teach yourself to move at a slower pace. You may even want to jot down some of the feelings you get in touch with in your journal. You'll be pleasantly surprised to discover that life is far richer when you stop to enjoy it.

### Listen to Your Wise Self

As you start to slow down and connect with how you feel, you're ready for another important ingredient in the practice of extreme self-care—reawakening the connection to your "Wise Self." You have an inner voice that, when listened to, will guide you to make decisions that are always in your best interest. Some refer to this voice as our higher self, inner wisdom, or intuition. I like to think of this voice as the voice of your soul, your Wise Self. It's the part of you that has more wisdom than you may be consciously aware of. It is your fundamental connection to the Divine, and when you listen and act on its wisdom your life becomes a magical journey.

Throughout this book, I'll ask you to call upon the guidance of your Wise Self to support you in making decisions. Over time, you'll come to rely on its wisdom in all that you do. I'd like you to begin opening this channel of communication with your Wise Self by trying the following exercises.

### Take Action! Ask for Simple Guidance

Throughout the day, stop and ask your Wise Self for guidance on specific simple decisions. Start with something small, like the best book to buy or the right movie to see. Pay attention to the answers that randomly pop into your mind. You may see an image, hear a voice, or feel a gut sense about the right choice to make. You may wonder if the choice is based on your Wise Self or just your imagination. Don't worry. Asking for guidance consistently sends a signal to your Wise Self that you're ready to pay attention. This opens the door to clearer communication. Over time, you'll find it easier to recognize the voice of your Wise Self; until then, just pay attention to what happens.

Amy was invited to see a movie with a friend. The movie was a drama about the early gangster days in Las Vegas. She had a gut instinct that it might not be the best choice. Amy hated watching violence and found it hard to forget the images in her mind long after such a movie was over. But, thinking that she was being too sensitive (a common judgment we make about our intuitive sense), she chose to go anyway.

Halfway through the movie, Amy felt sick as a particularly graphic violent scene took place. And for the rest of the movie it didn't get any better—instead, she felt progressively worse. By the end, she said she felt "violated" by the horrible images of brutality. When they left the theater, Amy was very upset. She felt angry at herself for not listening to her gut instinct (her Wise Self), but she had learned a valuable lesson, one she wouldn't forget. Amy's powerful emotional response served as a strong reminder that her Wise Self could be trusted.

Stop and ask your Wise Self for guidance on a simple decision now. Pay attention to the signals and be sure to act on its wisdom.

USE YOUR JOURNAL. For those of you who would rather try a different approach, writing letters to your Wise Self is another effective way to establish a connection. Using your journal, start by writing a letter that begins with "Dear Wise Self" and say whatever comes to mind. Let your thoughts flow easily without editing. Write until you feel complete. Then finish the letter by asking your Wise Self a question, such as:

- What's the best choice for me to make?
- What's the best direction for me to head in?
- What's standing in the way of my moving forward?
- What do I need to learn?

Focus your energy on this question as you write it down. Sit quietly and enter into a receptive state. You can do this by imagining an empty bowl in your mind just waiting for the answer. Or you can remember a time when you felt deep love. As you feel your heart and mind opening, quietly wait for a response.

When it feels right, slowly begin writing again. Let whatever comes to mind fill the page. In the beginning, you may hear your inner critic say things like "This is foolish" or "This is just my mind making up answers." It *is you* creating the answers, but as you connect with your Wise Self, your answers will be of a higher nature.

USE YOUR DREAMS. Paying attention to your dreams is another way of connecting with your Wise Self. Everyone has dreams, although we may not remember them. By writing your dreams in a journal, even just the fragments you remember, your unconscious begins to get the message that you are listening. When this message is received you'll find yourself remembering more of your dreams.

Before going to sleep, ask your Wise Self for guidance on a particular issue. Slowly bring your question into mind and hold it while drifting off to sleep. You may want to have a small tape recorder nearby to record any thoughts or impressions that may awaken you in the middle of the night. Since it's much easier to remember dream fragments when you can awaken slowly, trying planning this exercise without the use of an alarm clock. Sometimes your dreams will provide you with important, subconscious insights.

My client Gary decided to use his dreams as a way to gain insight on why he kept getting sick. Each night he asked his Wise Self the simple question, "What do I need to learn?" The first two nights, Gary could not remember any dreams, but he continued to ask the question. The third night, he had a very powerful dream. In his dream he witnessed the beating of a horse by a man who felt familiar, although he couldn't identify him. As he watched the man beating this horse, he found himself unable to speak. He wanted to stop him but couldn't say a word. When Gary and I discussed this dream and what it meant to him, he said that he felt that the horse and the man beating it both represented aspects of himself. Gary felt that the dream was telling him to put a stop to the way he constantly beat himself up.

### Take Action! Ask Out Loud

The last method of listening to your Wise Self is my favorite. When you find yourself faced with a dilemma or question, stand up and ask your Wise Self for help—out loud. For example, if you need help with how to proceed with a particular project, stand up and, using a firm voice, say: "OK, Wise Self, I need your help with this project. I'm stuck and I don't know how to move forward. What should I do?"

Notice the first thing that comes to mind. Does a person's name pop into your head, a piece of information or a place to go? Nothing? Whatever the response, follow through with action. Call the person you thought of and ask for help, follow up on the piece of information, go to the place that popped into your mind, or, if the response was nothing, stop what you're doing and relax.

As you start to rely on your Wise Self for guidance, you'll find yourself naturally making the best choices for your life. Stay open, listen for your inner voice, and, most important—act on it!

———

Congratulations! Now it's time to reward yourself for your hard work and dedication to you! Give yourself a gift. Schedule a massage, take the afternoon off and have some fun, see a good movie, or do something that acknowledges your decision to put yourself first. You're on the path to extreme self-care and beginning to put in place the habits that will help you to balance your life. These actions will get you started, and, as you incorporate this philosophy into your daily life, you'll find that "coincidences" start happening to you. As a higher order falls into place and supports your decision to take good care of yourself, write about these experiences in your journal and circle them in red! Let them remind you of the magic that occurs when you practice extreme self-care.

## COACHING REMINDERS
*Your life is not your work. Put yourself at the top of your "to do" list, and let the practice of extreme self-care build you a strong foundation for a high-quality life.*

- Start being selfish—you deserve it!
- Practice extreme self-care:
    Get to know your self!
    Connect your head with your heart.
    Listen to your Wise Self.

# RESOURCES

## *JOURNALS*

**Closerie Publishing, Inc.**
1952 South La Cienega Blvd.
Los Angeles, CA 90034
(310) 559–9704
> Closerie offers various kinds of blank journals.

**Running Rhino & Co.**
P.O. Box 24843
Seattle, WA 98124
(206) 284–2868
www.runningrhino.com
> Running Rhino sells various-sized blank, wirebound journals (Rhino Journals)—great for writing and drawing.

***SARK's Play!Book and Journal: A Place to Dream While Awake.***
SARK (Berkeley, CA: Celestial Arts, 1993)
> This unique journal prompts you to write by using fun and interesting questions.

## *WEB SITES*

**Dream Work: Dream Practices from Various Traditions**
www.resonate.org/places/practice/dreams.htm
> This Web site provides various information on dream work.

## *OTHER*

**Center for Jung Studies of Detroit**
17150 Kercheval Avenue
Grosse Pointe, MI 48230
(313) 881–7970
> This organization offers programs on dream studies.

*Inner Work: Using Dreams and Active Imagination for Personal Growth*
by Robert A. Johnson (HarperSanFrancisco, 1989)

Noted author and Jungian analyst Robert Johnson shows how working with your dreams and active imagination can integrate your conscious and unconscious selves, leading you to wholeness and a more satisfying life.

**Wayne McEwing**
The Dream Connection
dreamcomm@aol.com
888–why dream

Wayne provides dream consultations nationally by telephone. He believes that dreams provide fresh information directly from a client's highest, most authentic self, and he helps his clients to use this wisdom in their daily lives.

# 2

---

# Get Your

# Priorities

# Straight

---

It's Monday morning and once again Don is rushing to get to work on time. For more weeks than he cares to remember, he's been unable to get to the gym before work, something he really wants to do. But sleepless nights caused by stress are making it hard for him to get up early enough. As the medical director of a busy health center, he sees more than thirty patients a day, in addition to having phone consultations and managing the administrative staff.

Don says he feels like his life is "wasting away." He daydreams about getting married and starting a family but can't imagine how he would fit a wife and children into his crazy schedule. Driving to work, Don wonders how he'll get through the day, with patient appointments and staff meetings scheduled back to back until 7 P.M. Once again he'll have to cancel his squash game with George, a friend whose patience is wearing thin. Don's fed up with never having enough time for what he wants to do. As he pulls up to a red light, he leans his head back, closes his eyes, and reminds himself for the hundredth time that this craziness has to end.

How many times have you felt like Don, frustrated because you were unable to find time to do the things that were important to you? Does going to the gym, having lunch with a friend, or even reading a good book feel like just another item on your never-ending "to do" list? How long has it been since you were able to enjoy a relaxing afternoon at a museum or a quiet evening snuggled in bed watching a video?

Every day, millions of Americans juggle work and personal obligations trying to get ahead and keep up with the pace of life. They work long hours and fit in personal errands like banking and shopping during lunch and weekends. They take classes for work, attend conferences, and tackle the latest technology, trying to keep ahead of the competition. E-mail, voice mail, regular mail, faxes and FedEx—the very things that were supposed to make their lives easier—pull at them for attention, forcing them to put the things that are personally important on the back burner. It's no wonder that books on simplicity have become so popular—the desire to end this madness is high.

You have a choice about how you live your life, about how you spend your time. You can either continue with the way things are and hope it gets better, or you can do something about it. In this chapter we'll continue on the path of extreme self-care by focusing on the three things you'll need to do to get your priorities straight.

First, we'll take a realistic look at how you spend your time now. What gets your attention and focus on a daily basis? By taking a close look at where you spend your time, you can see clearly how you've defined your current priorities. You can then ask yourself whether these priorities make sense. Seeing your schedule from a new perspective highlights the changes you'll need to make to give up the juggling act and enjoy your life.

Once you've identified your current priorities, I'll ask you to call upon the guidance of your Wise Self to help you set new ones. By following your inner wisdom, you'll intentionally reorder your priorities or set new ones so that you can shift your focus and attention to what's important. Finally, once you've set your new priorities, I'll show you how to honor them so you can take time for your life.

## WHERE DOES ALL THE TIME GO?

Let's start by reviewing your schedule. Where do you spend your time? What does a typical week look like in your life? This is when my clients start to get nervous. When I ask them to fax me copies of their calendars so we can review a typical week, I immediately begin hearing the excuses for why they can't cancel a thing: "This is the third time I've rescheduled dinner, if I cancel again she'll kill me," or, "I've made a commitment to be at this meeting, I can't possibly back out now," and, "I'm the vice president of the board, it's my duty to be available at meetings twice a week." The underlying message in each of these very real excuses is that these people think they have no choice about how they use their time. That's where we make our first mistake—believing this lie.

We all have choices. Some of them may be very difficult, like breaking a commitment or canceling an appointment, leaving a job that demands too much, ending a relationship that drains your energy, or saying no to a child's request. But don't confuse tough choices with no choices.

If you want a quick and dramatic improvement in the quality of your life, make a big choice. For example, you may decide to resign as the vice president of the board and let someone else take over. Sure, the decision may be hard and you may be concerned with the reaction of others, but the quality of your life will be upgraded immediately.

Or, if you prefer a slower change of pace, make a smaller choice.

Cancel your appointments for an afternoon and do something fun, or reduce your stress level by keeping one night totally free to relax during the week. The point is, you have choices about how to live your life—it's just a question of how ready, willing, and able you are to make them.

Time is finite. You only get a certain amount—168 hours a week, fifty-two weeks a year, and that's if you're lucky. Time is a gift that most of us take for granted. We get so caught up in the busyness of our daily lives that we rarely stop and take a serious look at how we're spending this gift. Instead, we use appointment books, electronic calendars, and other elaborate tools in the hope of scheduling our time more efficiently. But these tools just perpetuate the myth that we can somehow "manage time." The truth is, we can only manage ourselves. The only way to truly make more time is to say no, schedule less, or cancel appointments. This is called "self-management," not time management.

New clients often complain that they find it impossible to fit in bathroom breaks, let alone a class they've always wanted to take or a relaxing conversation with a friend. When I look at the average time spent on normal activities during a typical day of week by those clients, it's no wonder their lives feel so out of control—there's literally not enough hours in the day.

| | |
|---|---|
| **Total hours available in one day:** | 24 |
| *Average time spent:* | |
| Sleeping (time spent in bed, not necessarily asleep) | 7 |
| Working (includes commute, prep, worry, etc.) | 12 |
| Life maintenance (eating, cleaning, errands, dressing, etc.) | 4 |
| Time to self (gym, time with friends and family, etc.) | 1 |
| Total hours left over | 0 |

With a schedule like this, weekends become a catchall for the necessities of life, like doing the laundry, getting your car or computer repaired, shopping for groceries, or doing other personal tasks, not to mention the work that inevitably gets taken home either in your briefcase or in your head. When you add up these hours over a week, it's even more telling.

One of the best ways to see whether your schedule reflects your priorities is to lay out on paper the details of a typical week's schedule. To get an idea of what I mean, let's look at the weekly schedule of my client Joan.

Joan is a married mother of two who is going to school full-time to complete her degree while raising her family. Her husband, a customer service engineer for a computer networking company, is on call twenty-four hours a day and rarely makes it home for dinner with the kids. Joan says her life feels chaotic. Between her kids' activities, school, and the care of her home, she lives in a constant state of overwhelm, which leaves her feeling exhausted most of the time.

During our call, Joan complained of feeling detached from her husband and easily frustrated by the kids. She questioned her original motivation for finishing school and reluctantly admitted that she had a secret fantasy of picking up and leaving this life behind.

Joan's fantasy is understandable, considering the condition of her daily life. I asked her to document how she spent her days, for one week. Once she completed this exercise, Joan's state of mind made perfect sense. Her schedule looked like this:

## JOAN'S TIME CHART

| Total Number of Hours Activities: | Sunday 24 | Monday 24 | Tuesday 24 | Wednesday 24 | Thursday 24 | Friday 24 | Saturday 24 | Total Hours 168 |
|---|---|---|---|---|---|---|---|---|
| Sleeping | 8 | 8 | 8 | 8 | 8 | 8 | 8 | 56 |
| School | 4 | 8 | 7 | 7 | 7 | 6 | 3 | 42 |
| Daily Tasks: | | | | | | | | |
| Grooming | 4 | 3 | 3 | 4 | 3 | 3 | 4 | 24 |
| Chores | | | | | | | | |
| Errands | | | | | | | | |
| Cooking | | | | | | | | |
| Laundry | | | | | | | | |
| Feeling Exhausted | 2 | 1 | 1 | 1 | 1 | 1 | 3 | 10 |
| Child Care | 4 | 3 | 4 | 4 | 4 | 3 | 4 | 26 |
| Husband | 1 | | | | | 1 | 1 | 3 |
| Self | 1 | 1 | 1 | | 1 | | 1 | 2 |
| Health | | | | | | 2 | | 3 |
| Friends | | | | | | | | 2 |
| Total Remaining Hours | 0 | 0 | 0 | 0 | 0 | 0 | 0 | 0 |

It's easy to see why Joan's life was so out of control. When she added in the average fifty-six hours a week spent sleeping, there were no hours left at the end of the week. Her school schedule, combined with managing the household and caring for her children, was more work than two people could handle. Joan, who was used to being in charge and on top of any situation, was now feeling out of control. This is typical, especially for high achievers. They'll keep doing and doing, handling it all, the way they always have, until finally they realize they can no longer make sanity out of an insane situation. Or they just burn out.

When you're immersed in a crazy schedule, it's easy to lose track of how you're spending your time and whether your priorities are out of order. When Joan listed her activities in order of priority based on the amount of time used, her priority list looked like this:

1. School (classes, commute, homework, study time)—42 hours per week
2. Daily tasks (grooming, cleaning, shopping, cooking, laundry, etc.)—24 hours per week
3. Time with children (care, fun time together, chauffeuring)—26 hours per week
4. Wasted time (feeling exhausted, depleted, and unable to do anything)—10 hours per week
5. Quality time with husband—3 hours per week
6. Quiet time to self (reading, relaxing)—2 hours per week
7. Emotional and physical health/time with friends—5 hours per week

Joan was surprised to see how little time she had for herself or her health and well-being. She wondered how things had gotten so out of hand. It's important to stop and take a close look at what's really taking your time. Often clients tell me that their family is a priority, yet when they review a week's schedule they find that they devote only three hours to that priority.

Later in this chapter we'll look at Joan's new priorities and see how she rearranged her schedule to honor them, but first let's find out where *your* time goes.

### Take Action! Where Does Your Time Go?

Where do you spend your gift of time? Using the blank time chart on page 61 as a guide, fill in your daily activities along with the average number of hours spent. Be creative—use a large piece of paper and give yourself plenty of room. Capture the details. If work is a major part of your life, you may want to break down your daily tasks to see if you're spending time doing what you most enjoy.

Be honest with yourself. For example, when you calculate your work time, be sure and add the actual time spent working to the time spent commuting, preparing for work, and worrying about work-related problems. When you total those hours, how much of your life is really taken up by your work?

If you use an appointment book, review several recent weeks to help you determine where your time goes. If you don't use an appointment book, ask your spouse, children, or close friends to give their impressions of what gets your time and attention. Sometimes I'll ask to speak with clients' spouses, roommates, secretaries, or co-workers to help my clients get a very clear picture of what they're doing during the week. These people can provide an excellent "reality check" and help you to recognize behaviors that you may be too busy to see.

In the left-hand column, list your activities using the examples below. Next, fill in the average time spent on each activity during the day. Then, total your hours for each day and the week.

## Activities List

Traveling
Studying
Worrying
Sleeping
Being entertained
Paying bills
Watching TV
Being alone
Personal grooming
Resting and relaxing
Responding to calls/e-mails
Being tired
Working (commute,
  preparation, worrying,
  creative thinking/
  imagining)

Commuting
Learning
Having fun
Shopping
Child caring
Being with friends or family
Volunteering
Participating in hobbies
Taking care of health and well-
  being
Taking part in spiritual practice
Reading
Daydreaming
Doing household chores
  (cleaning, cooking,
  errands, repairs/
  maintenance)

## MY TIME CHART

| Activities: | Sunday | Monday | Tuesday | Wednesday | Thursday | Friday | Saturday | Total Hours |
|---|---|---|---|---|---|---|---|---|
| **Total Number of Hours** | 24 | 24 | 24 | 24 | 24 | 24 | 24 | 168 |
| Sleeping | | | | | | | | |
| Work: | | | | | | | | |
| Commute | | | | | | | | |
| Preparation | | | | | | | | |
| Worrying | | | | | | | | |
| Daily Tasks: | | | | | | | | |
| Grooming | | | | | | | | |
| Chores | | | | | | | | |
| Errands | | | | | | | | |
| Cooking | | | | | | | | |
| Laundry | | | | | | | | |
| Other: | | | | | | | | |

**Total Remaining Hours**

### *Take Action! List Your Current Priorities*

How you spend your time reveals your true priorities. You can begin to see what you call important by how many hours you devote to that activity. Below, list the top seven things that take up most of your time. Using the total hours from your time chart, list your current priorities, beginning with the item that gets the most time and ending with the item that gets the least.

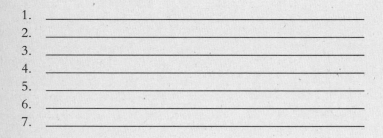

1. _____
2. _____
3. _____
4. _____
5. _____
6. _____
7. _____

As you review the list, ask yourself the following questions. Write the answers in your journal.

1. Am I living a balanced life?
2. What's missing from this list?
3. If this week were my last week on earth, would I be happy with how I'm spending my time?
4. Are my priorities what I thought they would be?
5. Are these the priorities that I most want?
6. How much of my time is spent caring for others?
7. Am I involved in too many activities?

Some clients actually find that they're missing time. In other words, their total hours add up to more than the 168 hours that are actually available in a week. Although this can happen as a result of estimating the hours, more often it's the result of a crazy schedule and a misconception of how time is spent.

### *Take Action! Define Your New Priorities*

Now that you've defined your current priorities—where you're spending your time—you're ready to reevaluate this list and consciously choose new priorities based on what's really important for your whole life. Your connection to your Wise Self is a crucial part of this planning.

Set aside an afternoon of uninterrupted time for this exercise. If you work out of your home, you may want to go somewhere else as a retreat from the inevitable interruptions that can occur. Think of this time as sacred, a time to go inside yourself and decide what you'll say yes to in your life.

Call upon your inner guidance to help design your new priorities. Start by putting yourself into a relaxed state. Close your eyes and breathe deeply, relaxing your body with each breath. Let your thoughts float freely.

When you're ready, open your journal and, using your current priority list, answer the following questions:

> *What's most important to you at this time in your life?*
> *Where would you like to spend more of your time?*
> *If you could do anything you wanted without restrictions, what would it be?*
> *Are there areas that need your attention, like your health, a relationship, work, or financial concerns?*
> *Is there a secret dream or desire that keeps getting put on the back burner that you'd like to devote more time to? If so, what is it?*
> *What needs less attention? More attention?*

Write the first answers that come to mind. Give yourself permission to let your desires run free. What do *you* want? Forget about the "shoulds," and focus on the "wants." What's important for your well-being and the next area of your personal growth? Are money problems keeping you tied to a job that you hate? Make it a priority to straighten them out. Would you like more fun in your life? Put it on the list. Is there a project you keep putting off, like writing a book or studying a foreign language? Write it down. Don't settle for less. This is your life. Choose the priorities that are personally important to you, and add them to the list. Consider all areas of your life:

> *Emotional and physical health*
> *Relationships*
> *Spiritual well-being*
> *Work*
> *Service/contributions to others*
> *Fun/adventure/leisure*

## Take Action! Create an Absolute Yes List

Once you've had a chance to define what's important, you're ready to create a new list—an Absolute Yes list. Your Absolute Yes list is a new list of priorities that will inspire you to use your gift of time differently. This list will become the governing document that will guide you to make wise choices about how you live your life. As an example, let's revisit Joan.

As Joan reworked her priorities, she realized that without making her emotional and physical health more important, she was headed for burnout and would be unable to care for herself or her family. She decided to move her self-care to the top of her new list and spend time each day reading, meditating, or giving herself permission to do absolutely nothing.

Since Joan felt strongly that a good marriage is a necessary foundation for raising children, she decided to make time with her husband next on the list. Not only would they spend time together during the week, but they decided to take one weekend every other month and go away overnight to a place they could easily afford. Many couples who work outside of the home find it easy to take the relationship for granted and end up losing touch with each other. Joan and her husband wanted to make the quality of their marriage a priority by spending more time together.

Joan also decided to cut back on the number of classes she took each semester. When redoing her list, she realized that the quality of her life was far more important than finishing her degree within a self-imposed deadline. By choosing her life over completing school quickly, she could enjoy both—a whole new concept.

Joan looked for ways to combine time with her family and time spent with friends. She and a girlfriend found activities to share with their children. I also recommended that she hire a housekeeper, even if it were only twice a month, to handle the household chores and laundry. And I encouraged her to give up control by allowing her husband to help out more with the kids. When Joan completed her new list, she felt an immediate sense of relief and excitement about the new focus of her time. Her new list looked like this:

1. Emotional and physical health—quiet time to herself, reading, daily meditation, and exercise
2. Relationship with husband—time together each evening before bed, date night during the week, one weekend away every other month
3. Relationship with children—care, fun time together, chauffeuring
4. School—attending classes, commuting, studying for exams
5. Time with friends—dinner, movies, cooking meals together
6. Household chores—shopping, cooking

It took Joan approximately six months to make the necessary changes to honor her priorities. She had to deal with her feelings of guilt about not being a good mother or wife when taking time for herself. But very quickly she realized that her self-care was the best way to care for her family. As a matter of fact, her husband and children began to comment on her good moods, and they actually welcomed the change. By reorienting her life around the things that were most important to her, Joan set a healthy example for her kids. It's been two years since Joan began working on her priorities, and as she is about to graduate and receive her degree, she's been very successful at keeping her priorities straight.

Now that you've spent time by yourself contemplating your new priorities, create your new Absolute Yes list below:

### My Absolute Yes List

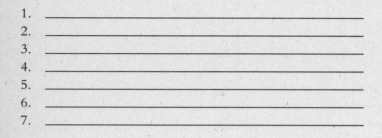

1. _____
2. _____
3. _____
4. _____
5. _____
6. _____
7. _____

Does this list excite you? Will it inspire you to shift your focus and give more of your attention to these areas? Now that you've completed the list, copy it onto several 3″-x-5″ index cards and keep these cards in view. Put one in your appointment book, one on your bathroom mirror, one on the dashboard of your car. Keep one by the phone so you're not tempted to agree to something that's not a priority. Let your Absolute Yes list remind you of what's important—what *you* really want. When you know what you want, your focus becomes crystal clear—you're able to honor your priorities in any situation.

## HONOR YOUR NEW PRIORITIES

Now that you know what your new priorities are, the next step is to honor them. I'd like to give you permission to reorient your life around what's most important to you. You can do this by using one or more of the following strategies:

- Bring your priorities into everyday life
- Learn to say no
- Schedule time for your life

### Take Action! Bring Your Priorities into Everyday Life

Let's start by shifting the way you think about how you spend your time. Instead of trying to "fit in" activities that reflect your priorities while your plate is full, look for ways to enhance your existing life with them. For example, if having fun is on your Absolute Yes list, look for ways to include fun in everyday tasks or events. My client Lindsay is a great example. When faced with a major challenge, she did a great job of honoring her priority of fun.

Lindsay and her husband decided that he would take a new position at a company located in a nearby state. Although the job would give them a $25,000 increase in annual salary, it posed one problem—they had three months to sell their home and move their family before the new school year began. It appeared that fate had dropped this new priority in Lindsay's lap to disrupt her life, but she chose to use it as an opportunity to get creative.

Lindsay had spent most of her life being too serious. When she redesigned her priorities, she decided to "lighten up," so she added fun to her list. To honor this priority, I asked Lindsay how she might make this impending move fun and easy. Immediately, ideas sprang to mind. Lindsay asked her family and friends to help her have fun while preparing to move. Several close friends agreed to bring their favorite music and plenty of boxes to a weekend sleepover "packing party." Next, she made a list of all the ways she had imagined improving on her current home and designed her next ideal place to live.

To make the move easy, Lindsay made a list of everything that needed to get done and began delegating the tasks. Her sister, a local realtor, offered to research the new area and provide realtors with Lindsay's wish list for her new home. Another friend offered to check into resources like babysitters, local schools, and health care providers. And Lindsay hired a team of college students to clean the house when the movers were done.

The move went surprisingly well. Lindsay made it a point to reward herself along the way as she completed various parts of the project. She scheduled massages and fun activities for herself and the kids. By involving her friends and family and making it fun, they were all able to enjoy their time together in special ways before she left.

With proper planning and creative thinking, almost any situation can be used as an opportunity to honor your priorities within the context of your daily life. As it was for Lindsay, fun was a priority for my client Bill. He developed an ideal client profile based on the characteristics of those clients who had been the most fun to work with and started saying no to anyone who didn't fit the bill. For the first time in years, he actually felt excited about getting to work.

My client Lois, an interior designer, made her spiritual well-being a high priority. In a bold move to bring this priority into her daily life, she shifted her business focus from traditional design to creating "soul nurturing" environments for her clients. Within a year, Lois became so well known for this specialty that she had to hire two assistants to handle the overflow of work.

How will you bring your priorities into your daily life? Review your Absolute Yes list and write three examples below. If you're unsure about how to do it, ask your coaching partner or group for their ideas.

1. _____
2. _____
3. _____

### Take Action! Say No Unless It's an Absolute Yes

Once you've determined what you want to say yes to, the ability to say no becomes an important muscle to build. An inability to use this muscle is the main obstacle that prevents most people from living the lives they want. This is why your Absolute Yes list must be filled with things that are truly important to you. When your priorities are compelling, it's great motivation to "just say no."

You decide what you will and won't do. If you don't say yes, the schedule doesn't fill. And if you say yes only to those things that you really want to do, you can avoid feeling frustrated or angry later on when you feel forced to do something you'd rather not do. A great way to tell how often you say yes when you mean no is to become aware of how you make decisions.

Over the next week, keep track of how many times you agree to something that's not a true yes—the kind of definite Yes! that you feel when invited to a favorite play or musical performance. Or notice how often you regret a commitment that you've already made, like agreeing to go to a social event that you'd rather not attend. Mark the number of times in your appointment book and total it at the end of the week. Now look at the number. Are you surprised?

If you're like most people, you probably find yourself saying yes to things that are not a priority for you. For example, you may agree to have dinner with a coworker simply because she's asked you several times and you feel obligated. You might take on an extra project at work, adding to your stress level, because you want to be seen as a hard worker. Or a family member calls in the middle of dinner and instead of telling him you'll call back and enjoying your meal, you stay on the phone and start to feel aggravated as the conversation drags on. These kinds of choices, often made quickly without much thought, will rob you of your precious gift of time.

Awareness is the first step. Pay attention to how often you do things that you'd rather not so you can start making decisions based on what *you* want. Use the Stop—Breathe—Feel exercise from chapter 1. Challenge yourself to put some space between a request of your time and your response. For many people, saying yes is an automatic response, an easier response. My client Sally was painfully familiar with this challenge.

Sally could always be counted on to say yes. She was the one her friends and family called upon when they needed help. For Sally, learning to say no was a scary proposition. She enjoyed being helpful and had come to rely on being needed by others—she said it made her feel loved. Sally was afraid that if she started saying no that people would get angry and stop calling her.

To make it easier, I asked Sally to let her friends and family know up front that, because of her new priorities, she would be saying no more often to their requests for support. This took faith on her part—by changing her behavior and making time to herself a priority, she risked losing these relationships.

When Sally informed her family and friends, she was surprised to hear that some of them not only understood her decision but wanted to support her as well. A couple of others naturally found someone else to bail them out, but something strange happened as Sally took care of herself: She didn't need or want those kinds of relationships anymore.

What stops you from saying no? When I ask my clients this question, I hear the following kinds of responses:

> *If I say no, I may disappoint others.*
> *If I say no, then I'll have to deal with the reactions that*
> *others may have.*
> *I'm afraid of rocking the boat and creating conflict.*
> *If I say no, I may regret it later.*
> *If I say no, people won't like me.*
> *If I say no, people may stop asking.*
> *If I say no, there may be serious consequences—someone may*
> *end our relationship or get angry, or I may lose my job.*
> *It's easier to just say yes.*

The common denominator in all these statements is fear. Saying no brings up a fear of disappointing or hurting others, missing opportunities, and making mistakes. But saying no means saying yes to you! Use your Absolute Yes cards as a guide. Keep them near you and refer to them often. Don't let the fear of saying no prevent you from living the life you want.

Use the following question as a guide to help you determine whether fear is stopping you from saying no to something in your life:

If you could say no to someone or something, knowing that there would be absolutely no hard feelings or negative consequences, who or what would you say no to?

Is there a project you would give up? A relationship you would end? A date you might break? Answering this question may reveal your true motivation behind those commitments you make and later regret. You may be more afraid of rocking the boat than of honoring your priorities.

Using the question above, make a list of five things you'd like to say no to:

1. _____
2. _____
3. _____
4. _____
5. _____

Next, ask your coaching partner or group for support. Start with the first no on your list and take action. It's OK to say no or change your mind, especially when you feel overwhelmed or pressed for time. There will be moments when creating a high-quality life will require you to disappoint others. Bear in mind that there is a spiritual principle that operates in life—when you take good care of yourself, it's always in the best interest of the other person as well. They may be disappointed or angry, but it doesn't make your decision to say no the wrong choice.

Like Sally, let others know up front that you've decided to honor your new priorities and that this may require you to change your mind. If it's not an absolute yes, then it's a no. Many clients are surprised to learn that changing their minds is a legitimate option. My client Jenny, a nurse at a big-city hospital, felt empowered by this choice.

Jenny had registered for a weekend conference with a friend. As the date approached, the idea of giving up a whole weekend after working four double shifts no longer appealed to her. Instead, she wanted to stay home and relax. When I suggested that Jenny cancel her registration and tell her friend that she had decided not to go, she seemed pleasantly surprised. She said it simply hadn't even occurred to her that she could cancel.

Jenny called her friend and explained the situation. When she told her that she really needed the weekend to relax and unwind, her friend was very disappointed and made no bones about telling her. Jenny held firm and decided not to go. The following week, over lunch, Jenny found out that her friend had met a man at the conference and had a terrific time.

In the beginning, you may need to make some difficult choices, like letting a friend down when you decide to cancel your plans, but soon, as you learn to make better decisions up front, the need to change your mind will happen less. For now, simply apologize and change your mind anyway.

One way to make changing your mind easier is to have the right words to say. Try using the following language:

"_____, I've realized that there's too much on my plate right now. I've made a commitment to be good to myself and I'll have to cancel our plans. I apologize for the change and hope you'll understand. Let's reschedule time a week from Monday."

How you deliver this message is just as important as what you say. Be direct and gracious. There's no need to overexplain. Stick with the truth—honoring yourself is always a valid excuse.

One way to avoid having to change your mind or disappoint

others is to give yourself room to breathe. When you're asked what time you can make a meeting, dinner, or any event, stop and add extra time to your first response. Or ask permission to change your mind beforehand. If you're not quite sure whether you want to participate, request the option to change your mind at the last minute.

Start making your commitments work for you. If you think you can finish a project in one week, say you'll need two, and deliver it early. Instead of using deadlines to motivate you, let a relaxed pace allow you to enjoy the process. This gives you room to breathe and helps you build a reputation as someone who keeps his or her word. After all, how many times have you found yourself engaged in a project that you originally felt excited about but became frustrated with because you waited until the last minute?

### Take Action! Schedule Time for Your Life

Building on your sacred date night from chapter 1, take out your calendar and for the next six months block out one afternoon or evening a week just for you (do this in ink). If you're self-employed, I usually recommend one full day a week—that way, if something important comes up you can default to an afternoon.

Spend this down time doing something you really enjoy. Let work go, and just have fun. Get a massage, see a movie, or visit a museum. Give yourself permission to shut your mind off! We all need a vacation from thinking too much. With schedules that are so structured and compartmentalized, we've lost touch with the joy of having nowhere to be. Schedule in "spontaneity breaks" at the end of the day when you have nothing waiting for you at the other end. Regular down time with nothing planned is essential to high-quality living and success.

By scheduling this kind of time beforehand, you protect yourself from overbooking. This deals with the source of the problem and helps you make decisions about future requests of your time. If it's blocked out for you, it's not available for anyone else. It's like canceling yourself from catalog lists instead of continuously throwing out all the catalogs you receive in the mail each day. Deal with the source of the problem. Take time for your life first.

I believe so strongly in regular down time that I often recommend it as a marketing strategy for my clients who own their own business. At first they think I'm a little crazy when I suggest that taking frequent breaks or vacations can actually bring business in the door. When I suggested this to my client Grace she laughed and said, "No way."

Grace is a terrific networker and is part of a powerful business community. Involved with three professional organizations, Grace loves being in charge and always helps out with fund-raising and planning events. When we started coaching, she complained that her business had reached a plateau and she wanted to take it to the next level.

When I reviewed a typical week, I saw that Grace had a very full schedule. She volunteered her time at least three nights per week, published a monthly newsletter, and always worked at least one day during the weekend. I suggested to Grace that if she wanted to build her business, she'd need to give up her volunteer activities for the next six months and block out two days per week in her schedule to take time for herself and for planning the next phase of her business. But she was reluctant to give up anything.

Instead, she agreed to cut back, and over the next three months Grace said no to several requests of her time. This felt awkward at first, but as she started to enjoy some space in her life, Grace saw how out of balance her priorities really were. As she got a taste of what life could be like without constantly running around, she started to cut back even more. Within three months, she resigned from two of her volunteer organizations.

When Grace reviewed her business at the end of the year, she was surprised to learn that her sales had increased by 20 percent while she was taking good care of herself. When you slow down, take time for your life, and practice extreme self-care, success always follows. Grace immediately planned her next vacation.

As you start saying no, you'll find that you have more time and space available in your calendar. The temptation will be to immediately fill the space. Don't get sucked in by the vacuum that having more time and space will create. Give yourself the gift of just "being" for a while. Many times, clients will complain that they feel bored with free time and anxious to fill it with something else. But your willingness to sit with the discomfort of boredom will allow you to get to the peace of mind waiting on the other side.

Intentionally practice doing nothing. Take daily breaks and allow yourself to just be. Start with a five-minute interval and sit quietly. If you'd like, imagine a place where you've felt deeply relaxed and let your mind rest there. When you find yourself getting antsy or uncomfortable, take a deep breath and bring your mind back to this place. Each day, add a minute to this exercise until you can sit comfortably for twenty or thirty minutes at a time. This simple exercise will teach you how to make peace with being instead of always doing. It's a great exercise to practice when you arrive early for a meeting, when you travel on the train, or anytime you're forced to wait.

My client Raymond, a fast-track entrepreneur, hated being bored. He always carried something to read or do in case he arrived early for an appointment, got stuck in traffic, or was forced to wait for someone else. The idea of doing nothing and simply being made him cringe. When he found himself with extra time on his hands, he agreed to humor me by playing a game I had heard about from a friend.

I asked Raymond to close his eyes and count backward from one hundred to eighty while visualizing each number in his mind's eye. Whenever his mind drifted away and caused him to no longer see the number, he had to start again from one hundred. Each day, he was to add ten counts to this number until he was able to get down to zero.

After practicing this exercise for three months, not only was Raymond able to get to zero, but he was now able to focus his attention in a powerful way. He called this game his new spiritual discipline.

Watch for the signs that indicate you're about to get pulled back into a busy life. When clients are starting to feel the discomfort of boredom or extra space, they say things like, "I think this might be a good time to start a new project." Or, "I feel like everyone else is moving ahead and I'm standing still." Or better yet, "I've been feeling sad and a bit lonely, I'm not sure what to do with myself." If you find yourself feeling the same way, you're in the right place. Let this be a sign to hang on through the boredom or discomfort until you get to the other side. When you can sit with space and extra time, you learn to fill it only with what's really important—those items on your Absolute Yes list.

Protect your priorities. Now that you know what's personally important to you, protect your new priorities by creating boundaries. Think of it as playing by new rules. For example, if peace of mind is a priority, implement a rule whereby you no longer answer your telephone after 9 P.M. or before 9 A.M. Setting this boundary will automatically help create a peaceful home environment. If maintaining a balance between your professional and personal life is important, decide to no longer conduct any business on the weekends. My client Rich, who has a home office, shuts his office door on Friday at 5 P.M. and does not enter it again until Monday at 10 A.M.

Think of these new rules as a way to create "protected" time and space for what's personally important to you. Jody, a client whose physical health is a top priority, no longer lets anything get in the way of her daily exercise regime. She's found the time of day that works best for her and has protected this time by scheduling work around it. Review your Absolute Yes list and ask yourself what new boundaries you'll need to set in order to insure that your priorities are protected. When you play by new rules, you create the life *you* want!

————

You deserve to live your life exactly the way you want. If you don't pilot your own plane, someone else will. Don't let others determine the quality of your life—take charge of that process yourself. Say no, change your mind, do whatever it takes to take time for your life. Let your Absolute Yes list become the governing document for the quality of your life. Reward yourself for the commitment and hard work you've done so far. Give yourself a day off!

COACHING REMINDERS
*You determine who and what gets your time. Choose wisely—your life depends on it!*

- Know where your time goes—how you spend your time reveals your true priorities.
- Decide what *you* want! Let your Wise Self guide you to set new priorities.
- Create your Absolute Yes list, and let it inspire you to live a great life!
- Honor your new priorities—bring them into your daily life, learn to say no, and, most of all, take time for you!

## RESOURCES

*BOOKS*

*First Things First: To Live, to Love, to Learn, to Leave a Legacy* by Stephen R. Covey, A. Roger Merrill, Rebecca Merrill (New York: Fireside Books, 1996)

*365 Ways to Simplify Your Work Life: Ideas That Bring More Time, Freedom and Satisfaction to Daily Work* by Odette Pollar (Chicago: Dearborn Trade, 1996)

***Time Shifting: Creating More Time for Your Life*** by Stephan Rechtschaffen
     (New York: Doubleday, 1997)
Rechtschaffen teaches the reader how to "time shift"—move in rhythm
with others, stretch the present, and practice mindfulness.

***The Circle of Simplicity—A Return to the Good Life*** by Cecile Andrews
     (New York: Harper Collins, 1997)
Andrews offers creative, practical ways to improve the quality of your life by
simplifying and changing your behaviors.

***Slowing Down to the Speed of Life*** by Richard Carlson, Joseph Bailey
     (Harper SanFrancisco, 1997)
A simple and powerful guide to creating a peaceful life from the inside out.


*MAGAZINE*

***Priorities Magazine—The Journal of Personal and Professional Success*** by
     Franklin Covey
In this bimonthly magazine, national contributors and experts offer advice
on career, family, communication, leadership, finance, health, and fitness.
To subscribe, call (800) 880–1492, or visit their online catalog at http://
www.franklincovey.com.

# 3

## What's

## Draining

## You?

Jody was my first client of the day. When I answered the phone, she could barely contain her excitement. Jody had really taken to the idea of extreme self-care and wanted to share a recent success. During our last coaching session I had introduced her to the idea of eliminating energy drains and had sent her a list, something I call the What's Draining You? checklist, to help her identify things that might be draining her energy. Already Jody had completed several items on the list, and one item in particular was responsible for her excitement.

Jody works for a film production company on the West Coast. For the last four years, in addition to her full-time job, she's been hard at work writing a screenplay. Most evenings she spent two to four hours drafting and fine-tuning this project. Six months earlier, Jody had completed the play and it had been collecting dust on her desk. For some reason, she couldn't bring herself to share the manuscript with the key individuals who could get it into the hands of someone who might produce it. Her boss had mentioned several times that he was willing to pass it along to a good friend, a successful movie producer, but she continued to thank him and ignore his offer.

After reading about energy drains, Jody realized that every day the manuscript sat on her desk it drained her energy bit by bit. As she completed some of the items on her checklist, she had a firsthand experience of the positive, powerful effect this had on her energy level and mood. She figured that since this project had been so important to her, she'd probably experience a hefty boost of energy by passing it along and completing the process.

Full of fear and excitement, one morning on the way out the door she lifted the manuscript from the desk and took it to work. At lunch, she handed it to her boss, expressed her concerns, and asked that he pass it along to his friend. Two days later, her boss informed her that his friend loved her project and wanted to schedule a meeting right away. Jody was overjoyed!

In the last chapter, we focused on redefining your priorities and what it takes to honor them in your everyday life. In this chapter, we'll focus on identifying and eliminating the things that drain your energy—the life energy that allows you to get things done, connect with others, and stay emotionally and physically fit. For most people who live stressful lives, this energy is limited and usually running close to empty.

Imagine that inside your body exists an inner barometer. Each day, as you go about your normal activities, the level of your inner barometer rises and falls according to the amount of energy you have available. When you work hard at a stressful job, you use up energy and the level decreases. When you eat a healthy meal, you add energy and the level increases. This barometer keeps track of where your energy level falls throughout the day. Normally we think of our energy levels rising and falling based on what we "do." But it's related to much more than that.

Every action you take uses energy. What you may not know is that actions you *don't* take use energy as well—mental energy, emotional energy, energy that could be used in a more positive way. The disorganized office you've been meaning to clean up distracts you and drains your energy. Clothing in need of updating or repair takes some of your energy each time you struggle to decide what to wear. The car overdue for an oil change zaps your energy every time you remember that it needs to be done. These things drain your energy in small ways each day.

And what about the more challenging ones? An elderly parent living far away whose issues cause you constant anxiety. The money problems you've been avoiding that awaken you in the middle of the night. Or the medical problem that gets put off until it becomes serious and unavoidable. These are just a few of the more debilitating energy drains that exhaust you and make it difficult to enjoy your life. These items on your mental "to do" list, the ones you've been proscrastinating about, distract you or make you feel guilty and drain the very energy you need to accomplish your goals.

How does this energy connection work? Caroline Myss, author of *Anatomy of the Spirit,* explains, "In the human energy system, our individual interactions with our environment can be thought of symbolically as electromagnetic circuits. These circuits run through our bodies and connect us to external objects and other people." She goes on to say that "we are constantly in communication with everything around us through this system."

Imagine for a moment that cords of energy run from your body to everything undone or incomplete in your life. These cords run from you to your past (what's left incomplete or unresolved) and your future, what you hope for and worry about. When these cords of energy become tied up in your past or your future (the places where most of us live), this leaves no energy available for the present.

Some cords are wider than others, representing those items that have more energy flowing to them (often the items that we fear the most, like the unfiled tax returns or the medical problem we've been avoiding). These energy cords pulsate with your life force, the same life force you need to stay healthy, enjoy friends and family, have fun, express yourself creatively, and do the work you love.

How many cords flow to areas that please you? How much energy do you have available in this present moment to do what you most want with your life? Stop for a moment and take out your journal. Take a few deep breaths to center yourself and relax. Now, notice where your energy flows. What are you worried about? Is your energy pulled back to a conversation with a coworker that made you angry last week? What have you been meaning to take care of? Is your will up to date, your taxes filed? Are you concerned about something in the future? Is there a conversation you need to have with your boss, a friend, or your mother? Notice what gets your attention and steals your precious life energy.

Now imagine that you can reroute those cords. By dealing with each item, with the right tools, you handle each one completely, slowly bringing your energy into present time. Imagine pulling all your energy back into the present moment. Feel yourself getting stronger, more energized, and excited about your life. How does it feel to have your full energy back? Do you feel a sense of relief and inner peace as you are freed from these things?

My clients are usually quite surprised to learn that a majority of our initial work together will be focused on *removing* things from their lives instead of achieving goals. Once again, it's all about extreme self-care. First you become selfish, then you start arranging your life to reflect your priorities, and then you identify and eliminate what drains you!

On the page opposite is the What's Draining You? checklist to help identify where your energy is being syphoned off. This list represents some of the common energy drains I've heard from my clients. Take a few minutes to review the list. Take a deep breath and invite your Wise Self to help you. Check the items that apply to you and feel free to add others that may occur to you.

## *Take Action! Pinpoint What Drains You*

### *What's Draining You?*

Relationships

_____ There are people in my life who continuously drain my energy.

_____ I have unreturned phone calls, e-mails, or letters that need to be handled.

_____ I have an unresolved conflict with a family member.

_____ I lack quality friendships in my life.

_____ I feel a void in my life created by the lack of a romantic partner.

_____ There is someone I need to forgive.

_____ There is a relationship I need to end.

_____ There is a phone call I dread making, and it causes me stress and anxiety.

_____ I'm currently involved in a relationship that compromises my values.

_____ I miss being a part of a loving and supportive community.

Environment

_____ My car is in need of cleaning and/or repair.

_____ My wardrobe needs updating and/or alterations.

_____ I'd like to live in a different geographic location.

_____ I have appliances that need repair or upgrading.

_____ My home is not decorated in a way that nurtures me.

_____ My closets and/or basement are cluttered and need to be cleaned.

_____ Repairs need to be done around my home or apartment.

_____ My home is cluttered and disorganized.

_____ I miss having more beauty reflected in my environment.

_____ I watch too much television.

### Body, Mind, and Spirit

_____ I eat food that's not good for me.

_____ Something about my physical appearance bothers me.

_____ It's been too long since I've been to the dentist.

_____ I do not get the sleep I need to feel fully rested.

_____ I'd like to exercise regularly but never seem to find the time.

_____ I have a health concern for which I've avoided getting help.

_____ I have emotional needs that consistently go unmet.

_____ There are books that I'd love to read but never seem to find the time for.

_____ I lack personal interests that are intellectually stimulating.

_____ I lack a spiritual or religious practice in my life.

### Work

_____ I no longer enjoy my job and have a hard time showing up each day.

_____ My work is stressful and leaves me exhausted at the end of the day.

_____ My office is disorganized, my desk is a mess, and I have trouble finding what I need.

_____ I'm avoiding a confrontation or conflict at work.

_____ I tolerate bad behavior from a boss or coworker.

_____ I am not computer literate, and it gets in the way of my productivity.

_____ I lack the proper office equipment that I need to do my job well.

_____ My work does not allow me to express my creativity.

_____ I know I need to delegate specific tasks but am unable to let go of control.

_____ I feel overwhelmed with the amount of information that enters my life in the form of mail, books, magazines, and e-mail.

*Money*

_____ I have tax returns that are not filed or taxes that are not paid.

_____ I pay my bills late.

_____ I spend more than I earn.

_____ I don't have a plan for my financial future.

_____ My credit rating is not what I'd like it to be.

_____ I do not have a regular savings plan.

_____ I do not have adequate insurance coverage.

_____ My mortgage rate is too high, and I need to refinance.

_____ I have debt that needs to be paid off.

_____ My will is not up to date.

Let's see where your energy is going. Value each item at 2 points. Tally each section individually and multiply the total by 2. Now combine the total scores of each section and see what you get. If you imagine that your inner barometer begins with 100 points, what's your level now? How much energy do you have left for what's really important? Are there areas that cause more energy drains than others? As we move through this chapter, write the score in your journal so you can keep track of how well you're eliminating your energy drains.

Can you *feel* the amount of mental energy being used by these items? If you're like most people, you probably have at least 75 percent of your mental energy tied up in these types of distractions. Most of us are unconscious about how our mental energy is used throughout our day-to-day lives. Becoming conscious of where your energy flows can be very revealing. It may startle you to realize that, while you have a very difficult boss, it's really the state of your finances that saps your strength.

Review the results of this checklist thoughtfully. Now that you're aware of what's draining you, you can begin to focus on handling the things you've been putting off or putting up with. It's a tremendous relief, in fact, to be able to take action. As you take care of the things that distract you and drain your energy, you'll immediately feel an energy boost—a great motivating force. You'll have more energy for the actions that support your priorities. Don't let the actions that are most important to your quality of life receive the least attention anymore. Plug those drains and restore your energy!

My client Ron was fed up with feeling drained. Thirty pounds overweight, he had tried exercise programs, a personal trainer, and the latest diet to help him get fit. Over the long run, nothing seemed to work. When we began our work together and Ron set new priorities, he put his physical health at the top of the list. He wanted to exercise consistently, a common item on clients' procrastination lists, but he kept putting it off. The constant hum of his negative self-talk about the need to get in shape was one of his biggest mental energy drains.

Most people find it hard to make the time to exercise regularly, even though they really want to. Inevitably, they fail to measure the amount of emotional and physical energy they have available to devote to their health. Without enough energy in your life, regular exercise becomes another "should" instead of a great way to reconnect with yourself and your body. Like everything else, we first need to make the energy connection.

I asked Ron to use the What's Draining You? checklist and create a Top-Ten Procrastination list to determine where his energy was being used. His list looked like this:

1. Exercise regularly and eat right—lose thirty pounds.
2. Clean out the garage before winter to fit the cars.
3. Spend more time with Dina [his wife] and the children.
4. Develop strategic plan for next year's business goals.
5. Finish painting the fence.
6. Read through the stacks of new product information on the floor in my office.
7. Hire two sales associates.
8. Make dentist and doctor appointments.
9. Clean out basement.
10. Cut back on my coffee and sugar intake.

As the owner of a fast-growing retail sports store, Ron worked at least seventy hours per week. This didn't account for the mental and

emotional time spent worrying about sales goals and employee problems, as well as focused strategic planning. All in all, Ron was ex-
pending at least 80 percent of his energy on the business, which
didn't leave much for his wife, three children, and household projects, let alone exercising. Without enough energy, he was doomed to
fail.

I encouraged Ron to take a different approach to accomplish his
number one priority. Explaining the energy connection, I suggested
that he first focus on removing any obstacles that were preventing
him from making his physical fitness a priority. As we reviewed his
procrastination list, we first looked for things that he could delegate
to others. I suggested that he hire someone to finish painting the
fence, have his employees review the new product information and
make recommendations, and use the support of a good nutritionist to
help him adjust his diet. Although Ron had some resistance to delegating, once he gave it a try he quickly got over the "nobody does it
better or quicker than me" trap.

Next we made those personal things that Ron had to do part of a
family game. This allowed him to spend more time with his family
*and* complete his projects. Ron enlisted the support of his wife and
kids to help him get organized and complete the household projects
that had been bothering him for some time. Together they kept track
of the things that needed to be completed on a chart they hung on
the kitchen wall. As they marked off an item, they found creative
ways to celebrate their success. Over the next six months, as Ron
completed the projects on his list, he experienced a sense of peace
and well-being that came from having more energy in his life. As this
energy returned, he found more time to exercise consistently and
naturally by taking walks with his wife and biking with his kids.

The commitment to make the difficult but necessary changes that
will restore your energy can have an immediate positive impact on
the quality of your life. Deciding to finally file for a divorce or leave a
job that no longer serves you can suddenly move you in a completely
new direction. As a matter of fact, this can be the very reason why
some people stay stuck and avoid taking action. Subconsciously, they

know that their lives will change as a result of completing things or letting go of old "stuff." I've watched clients overcome a lifelong fear of doctors by finally getting a checkup and then make a move cross-country to a location they've always wanted to live once they've received a clean bill of health. I've seen them end an unhealthy relationship and attract a new, healthy partner once they've faced their fear of being alone and improved their own well-being.

What life changes might you experience if you begin to eliminate your energy drains? Ask yourself whether you're holding back from handling things because of how it might impact your life.

―――――

Now that you've identified some of the areas that might be draining your energy and distorting the balance of your whole life, it's time to create your own Top-Ten Procrastination list. Here's how you begin:

1. Review the items you've checked in the What's Draining You? list.
2. Make a list of any items you've added to the checklist.
3. As you review them, choose ten items that you'd most like to handle now and list them below.

*My Top-Ten Procrastination List*

1. _____
2. _____
3. _____
4. _____
5. _____
6. _____
7. _____
8. _____
9. _____
10. _____

When my client Katherine took the What's Draining You? test and created her Top-Ten Procrastination list, she was amazed at how much of her energy was invested in things that were distracting her from her priorities. As the president of a training and development firm, she constantly juggled her schedule to meet the meeds of her clients. She had very little time to relax and often felt lonely and isolated. After reevaluating her priorities, Katherine realized how important it was to her to begin an intimate relationship that would lead to marriage and a family.

As we looked closely at her life, it was clear that she did not have the energy for a relationship. Her weekdays were spent traveling throughout the country, and she needed her weekends to recover from the stress of her work. I pointed out that without enough time for herself, she had no time for a relationship. And besides, in her state it was likely that she would attract a man who was unavailable too!

Katherine noticed that she scored high in the work, environment, and health sections. Because of her crazy travel schedule, she wasn't home much and had not created a nurturing environment in which to live. She also spent too much time on airplanes and in hotels breathing bad air and eating unhealthy food.

Katherine decided to make her personal life the focus of her energy and attention first instead of finding the right man. She cut back her hours by training her staff to replace her in 50 percent of the work she was involved in. This allowed her to reduce her travel schedule and begin taking good care of herself. Wanting to create an environment where she felt nurtured, Katherine found a decorator to help redesign her home. She also found a food service that would deliver healthy meals.

Within eight months, Katherine felt more at peace with her life. She spent much more time in her newly decorated home and had far more energy for fun on the weekends. As her energy returned and she felt better about herself, I suggested that she begin creating an "ideal partner" profile. Each day, while writing in her journal, she should list the qualities she desired in a life partner. It was no coincidence that one month later she started to meet men who fit this profile and began dating again for the first time in three years.

### Take Action! Restore Your Life Energy

Now it's time for you to act on those things that are draining your energy once and for all. Make several copies of your top-ten list and put them where you can review them on a regular basis. Keep one in your office, one in your appointment book, and one on the kitchen wall or refrigerator.

Next, assign a time frame for when you'll complete the full list. I usually recommend thirty days, depending on what needs to be done. Some things—like making appointments with professionals, developing new friendships, and changing geographic locations—will require more time. You can begin taking action by making the necessary appointments, creating a list of qualities you'd like in a new friend, or researching the areas where you'd like to live.

Generally speaking, there are three ways to complete the items on your list:

> *Take care of it yourself. Do it!*
> *Transfer the task to someone else. Hire it!*
> *Throw it out. Chuck it!*

### Do It!

This method is for things only *you* can do, like dealing with health issues, addressing relationship problems, or moving to a new location (although you can get lots of help with the move). Review your list and schedule time in your appointment book to handle these particular items in a focused and structured way. Too often we make these things the last priority, even though they take a tremendous amount of energy. Set aside a day or an afternoon, and start getting things handled!

For example, the amount of energy used in holding back the truth and avoiding conflict is significant. The relief that comes afterward is amazing—you can actually feel the energy release. Be sure and get support! With your partner or coaching group, hold a "tell the truth" day. Have everyone commit to telling their truths by a certain time, and then plan to report back on your experiences.

When a client is having a difficult time getting up the courage to tell the truth, I usually offer to speak with them before and after the event. It's much easier to approach a potentially difficult situation knowing that there is someone waiting to support you when you're done. My client Patricia found this kind of support helpful in dealing with a business partner with whom she could no longer work.

She and her partner had been together for more than ten years, and she knew it was time to end their relationship. They had grown in different directions, and tensions were mounting between them. She felt blocked by her fear and unable to tell him the truth. Patricia needed three things to move forward. First, she needed help with what to say—she needed the language. Second, she needed support waiting for her on the other end of the conversation—someone she could debrief with afterward. And finally, she wanted to deliver her message in a way that would honor their relationship.

Using the "I" context, I helped Patricia script a conversation and had her practice it with me until she could deliver it naturally. Starting the conversation with "I" helps to put the emphasis on you and not on who the other person is or what they have done. This makes for respectful communication and helps honor the relationship. It's always smart to write out any important conversation and to practice it with a neutral party. This will help you to think it through and feel confident when the time comes to share it with the appropriate person.

When Patricia called me after her meeting with this partner, she felt shaky but relieved. Her partner was not surprised, and although he was upset and disappointed, she felt the conversation had gone better than expected.

Telling the truth with grace and love is always possible with preparation and support. Remember, get help with what to say, don't overexplain, stick to the truth, and always start with "I" statements.

If handling a health issue (like going to the doctor or dentist) makes you anxious, interview healthcare providers and choose only those who are sensitive to your needs. Ask a friend to go with you. Don't do scary things alone!

Think of this process as a way to create space for better things to come into your life. The "stuff" we hold onto, either in our head or in our environment, takes up space that could be available for new opportunities, great people, additional business, or even more money. I introduced this concept to Peter, a client with a pile problem.

Peter was a busy trial attorney who had more cases than he could handle. Adding to his stress were filing cabinets overstuffed with papers and piles of client folders spread across his office floor. Peter said that each day when he entered his office he felt instantly weighted down by the sight of the mess.

Although Peter was anxious to get organized, he had not made the time to purchase new filing cabinets. I challenged him to call a local used office furniture store that afternoon and have three cabinets delivered, one more than he thought he might need. That way, with an extra cabinet, he'd have a reserve of space. I explained to him that cleaning out his files and creating order from chaos was actually a smart business move. By clearing the space in his office, he was clearing the space in his mind and, as a result, would improve his performance dramatically, leaving his clients feeling well served.

When the cabinets were delivered, Peter felt prompted to schedule an afternoon to handle the mess. He used his afternoon appointment to completely reorganize his office. Not only did he put all the files away, he also installed two shelves to display his favorite photographs and professional awards, something he had wanted to do for over a year. When I asked Peter why he went beyond clearing up the piles, he replied, "I was on a roll. Once the papers were filed, I was so excited by the extra space that I decided to keep going until the office looked great!" Now when he enters his new office, he no longer feels drained. Instead, he feels energized and ready to get things done.

Everyone I've ever worked with has felt a great sense of relief when they complete the tasks that have been hanging over their heads. Now, when clients want suggestions on how to achieve their goals—like increasing their business, meeting a new partner, or making a new friend—I tell them to clean out a filing cabinet or empty a closet. They laugh, but I know that "if you make the space, they will come."

Once you've completed the items on your list that you have to do, go back and check them off. Then total your score on the What's Draining You? list again and imagine the energy level rising on your inner barometer. Doesn't it feel great to get these things handled? Can you feel the energy? The relief? Great! Now let's move on to the next method—letting someone else do it!

## HIRE IT!

This is my favorite method of eliminating what drains you. Find someone else to clean the car, run your errands, organize your office, or handle your bookkeeping. In our busy lives, this is a primary way to remain sane and spiritually balanced. Having someone else handle the problems on your list is a fast and easy way to get things done. You may resist letting someone else do things for you, but get over it! If you can't afford to pay for the support, then barter. "No one can do it better or faster than me" and "it will take me longer to teach someone than to do it myself" are frequent excuses I hear that keep my clients stuck or feeling overwhelmed. Share the wealth and employ someone else to free up your time and energy—your peace of mind is worth the investment!

Hiring an assistant is a good example of the kind of "hire it" obstacle that gets in the way of my clients' success. Justin, a bright young accountant, knew it was time to hire a personal assistant long before he actually did it. He had three major concerns when he considered bringing someone on board. Could he afford it? How would he find the time to train someone when he was already too swamped? Would his clients feel comfortable dealing with someone else?

To motivate him to explore this option further, we looked at what his time was worth. Justin was a self-employed CPA who charged $125 per hour for his services. Although he had a receptionist, he often had to schedule meetings and conference calls and conduct research for his clients. When Justin realized that it was costing him $125 per hour to do these things, he had to ask himself a new question. Could he afford *not* to hire someone?

I introduced Justin to the idea of working with a new kind of assistant—a "virtual assistant." This virtual assistant would work out of her home, on her own computer, and charge him only for the time she worked. This eliminated the cost of setting up another office (furniture, computer, phones, etc.) and paying someone for time that wasn't being used. Next came his concerns about training and whether his clients would feel uncomfortable dealing with someone other than himself. I suggested that Justin put in writing exactly what he wanted in a new assistant, both professionally and personally. He would have to interview carefully to find someone well suited to his personality and style. By using the services of a highly competent and personable assistant, one who would learn very quickly, his clients would actually be better served. After all, Justin was under a great deal of pressure and I was sure that his clients could tell.

There was a catch to using a top-notch assistant—he had to be willing to pay well for this kind of support. Most people try to skimp on the cost and end up shortchanging themselves. Yet an investment in a high-quality assistant would pay for itself, usually within thirty days. Justin agreed to a trial period, and at the end of one month, with client requests handled in half the time, he wondered how he had ever lived without his new virtual assistant.

If you're unsure about whether it's time to hire someone to support you, try this exercise. For the next two weeks, keep a pad of paper nearby and each time you find yourself completing a task that someone else could do, write it on the list. Whether you're a homemaker or CEO doesn't matter—pay attention to the things you no longer enjoy doing and add them to the list. Just the simple act of having someone take over your laundry duties or the grocery shopping or having your car repaired can free up an enormous amount of energy.

Determine the tasks to be done and decide what type of person is best suited to do the job. If it's a simple matter of running errands or doing work around the yard, a student might be the perfect choice. Post an advertisement on the bulletin board at your local university student center, or ask a neighbor's son or daughter. Or, consider hiring your own children. If it's more involved—like reorganizing your office space or creating a database—you'll want to hire more experienced support, like a professional organizer, secretary, or virtual assistant. If you're unsure, ask for help. Think about friends and colleagues who have great support people in their lives and have them help you make the best choice. I've provided resources at the end of the chapter to help you find the right support.

Once you've delegated the appropriate items on your list, go back again and check them off. Total your score and feel your energy level increase once again. By now you should find yourself so motivated that you're ready for the last step—let it go!

## CHUCK IT!

Sometimes we keep tasks on our "to do" list that just need to be dropped. The need to go through each and every magazine before throwing it out may be unnecessary. Just get rid of them. Or the clothes that need repair, that you *might* wear again (although it's been years), may just need to be given away. Challenge yourself to let go whenever possible. If you're afraid that you may need something once it's gone, there are three things you can do to help alleviate this fear:

1. Box up any paperwork or items that you're not yet ready to let go of and date it six months from now. Note this date on your calendar. Put this box in your basement or storage area. If, after six months, you've not gone into the box, throw it out *without* looking inside. This will teach you to throw things out sooner rather than later.

2. Determine where you'd find something if you needed it. Before you throw something out, ask yourself, "Where could I find this again if I needed it?" This way, you'll know ahead of time that it's not lost forever. With the amount of information now available on the Internet, you're almost sure to find whatever you need. If you don't believe me, spend an hour surfing the Web. If you don't have your own access, visit your local library or cybercafe and take some time to notice how much information is available. You'll be amazed at what can be found this way. Seeing what's out there can help reassure you that you'll be able to access whatever you need when you need it.

3. Ask for help. Going through piles of paperwork, old files, and magazines can be overwhelming or boring. Ease the pain. Invite a friend over and have a "pile party." Ask for support in throwing out things you're reluctant to part with. Choose a friend who is much better at organizing and throwing things away and ask him to sit with you and help you to decide what to keep and what to chuck. Remember, you're making space for much better things. With your new priorities in mind, ask yourself this question: Am I willing to let this item take up the space for what I really want (more business, new relationships, more abundance)? When you find yourself on the fence about whether to throw something out, this question can be a great filter for making a decision.

Donate the things you no longer need. Plenty of organizations (like Salvation Army and Goodwill) are always looking for household items and clothing for the needy. The opportunity to give to someone else can be a great motivating force for you and your family. When my client Maura was having a hard time getting her family to part with their unused items, I suggested that she do some research and learn as much as she could about a local shelter. Once she had more information about the kinds of people this shelter supported, I asked her to call a family meeting and share the details with her family. This brought the needs of the shelter "close to home" and encouraged her family to become personally invested in helping out.

The following Saturday, they spent five hours going through the house from top to bottom gathering all they no longer used. Together as a family, they made three trips to the shelter to deliver their gifts. Schedule your own "give away" day—it not only helps to create space but allows your children to experience how good it feels to give to others. And remember, it's a tax deduction too!

Hold a garage sale or yard sale and make some extra money. It's still true that one person's junk is another person's treasure. One of my clients holds a neighborhood yard sale every year and makes over $1,000! Find a local consignment shop and sell the clothes you no longer wear. Donate your old books to your local library—that way, you can always find them when you need them.

Avoid clutter buildup. Look for the source of the problem. For example, if you have a post office box, go through your mail at the post office and throw every scrap of paper away. Make it a game to bring home only what you absolutely need. Schedule one afternoon each week to scan your home or office with the intent to throw out or handle anything that's hanging around. Teach yourself to follow through and handle paper only once by using a simple mantra when you're about to stop in the middle of completing a task. Repeat to yourself: "I always do complete work," and finish the job.

Hold a swap party. Every six months, my client Kelly and her friends get together to exchange clothes, jewelry, and household items they no longer use. Each of them always finds a treasure or two during this event, and, if any items are left over, they donate the rest to charity.

Say good-bye to all that you no longer need. Go back to your Top-Ten Procrastination list and check off the additional items you've completed and then retotal your score. Congratulations! You're well on your way to having more energy for what really matters!

———

As you go through the process of completing the items on your list, look for ways to make it fun. For example, when I was writing this book, I often listened to music that inspired me. Sometimes it was loud and funky, and other times it was slow and calming. Sometimes I stopped in the middle of a page when I felt stuck or frustrated and did something completely different, like reading a chapter from a favorite novel or singing at the top of my lungs. Then I'd go back to writing. What can you do to make the process of raising your energy level more enjoyable?

Finally, be sure and reward yourself along the way as you eliminate your energy drains. Knowing that you'll be able to enjoy dinner with a friend, a good movie, or simply time to relax with your favorite book can be a great motivating force.

## Procrastination—A Gift in Disguise?

As a final thought, there may be times when procrastination serves as a messenger for subconscious insights and information. If you find an item on your list that you just can't get done, you may realize, like my client Leah did, that there is an important reason why.

Leah lived amidst piles of paper scattered throughout her apartment. She had tried several times over the last three years to tackle the piles, but something seemed to get in the way of letting them go. Leah kept beating herself up for not completing this task. Using my intuition, I decided to take an unconventional approach. I asked Leah to find an evening when she could arrange to be alone with uninterrupted time. I then instructed her to light candles around the piles on the floor, sit among them, and ask for the wisdom and insight that they might have to offer. Yes, Leah did question my sanity for a moment but decided to give it a try. What happened was pretty amazing.

As she looked around at the piles strewn among the flickering candlelight, she felt overwhelmed with a deep sadness. Suddenly she understood why she couldn't let them go. Scattered throughout the piles of paperwork were notes for a book that Leah longed to write.

As she connected with this unmet dream, Leah began to sob uncontrollably. She now knew why the piles wouldn't go away—they were there as a gift to keep her dream of writing alive. That evening, Leah took out her appointment book and scheduled time to write every day. Through her commitment to honor her creative spirit, the piles naturally began to disappear.

Is there something that you've resisted taking care of? As you think about the items you can't seem to complete, consider the following questions:

> *Am I sabotaging my success in some area of my life by not completing things?*
> *What message does this resistance hold for me?*
> *How does holding onto this task serve me?*
> *What could I do to honor the resistance?*

Look to see what gift may lie behind those items that you can't seem to complete.

---

Review your procrastination list and the What's Draining You? checklist. Imagine a life where all these items are handled for good. How much more energy would you have to dedicate to your priorities? What if you could actually accomplish your goals by eliminating all the things that distract or drain your energy? Sound strange? Try it. I'm convinced that, like many of my clients, you'll find that creating the space can actually *attract* what you most want into your life.

Next we'll deal with the biggest energy drain of all—money problems.

## COACHING REMINDERS
*When you eliminate what drains you, you make the space for what's really important.*

- Energy is *the* ingredient for success. You decide who/what gets it. Choose wisely!
- Create your Top-Ten Procrastination list and get to work!
- Stop managing chaos. Eliminate it! Do it! Hire it! Chuck it!

## RESOURCES

### PROFESSIONAL ORGANIZERS

**National Association of Professional Organizers**
http://www.napo.net
(512) 206–0151

> To find a professional organizer near you, contact the National Association of Professional Organizers, a nationwide network of professionals in all areas of organization. They offer a referral service via e-mail.

### OFFICE EQUIPMENT AND SUPPLIES

**Office Depot**
(800) 685–8800

**Office Max**
http://www.officemax.com
(800) 788–8080

**Staples**
http://www.staples.com
(800) 333–3330

### OFFICE SUPPORT AND PROFESSIONAL ASSISTANCE

**International Association of Administrative Professionals**
http://www.psi.org
(816) 891–6600

## VIRTUAL ASSISTANTS

### Assist U
http://www.assistu.com
(410) 666–5900

This organization offers training for virtual assistants and refers qualified VAs.

## OTHER

### Zero Junk Mail
http://www.zerojunkmail.com
(888) 970–JUNK (5865)

Zero Junk Mail is the premier service dedicated to stopping the flood of intrusive telemarketing calls, junk mail, and junk e-mail that is invading your life.

### *How to Have Big Money Garage Sales and Yard Sales*
http://win-edge.com/GarageSales.shtml
(800) 841–4248

You can order a manual from this site that provides tips that guarantee to triple your garage or yard sale income.

To find garage sales in your community and to list yours free: http://garagesale.nearu.com

For information on a national listing of flea markets, contact:
### Flea Market Guide of U.S. Flea Markets
http://www.bargain-mall.com/fleas.htm

### Salvation Army
http://www.salvationarmy.org
(800) 95–Truck

### Goodwill
http://www.goodwill.org
(301) 530–6500

To place a free ad for things the average family needs to get rid of, contact:
**Classifieds 2000**
http://www.classifieds2000.com

## BOOKS

**Simple Abundance: A Daybook of Comfort and Joy** by Sarah Ban Breathnach
(New York: Warner Books, 1995)
A practical, inspirational daily guide that provides a meditation or exercise
for every day of the year to help women pare down their lives and clear their
mental clutter.

**Anatomy of the Spirit** by Caroline Myss (New York: Harmony Books,
1996)
A great resource for understanding a different view of how our life energy is
used and a bold presentation of the emerging field of energy medicine.

**The Simple Living Guide** by Janet Luhrs (New York: Broadway Books,
1997)
An excellent resource for creating a simpler, more fulfilling life.

## HOME SERVICES

**www.peapod.com**
An online grocery service that will deliver to your home.

**Merry Maids**
1 (800) WESERVE
A nationwide cleaning service. Call to get local rates.

**Diet Pik-Up**
(888) 344–DIET
Will find a distributor in your area to deliver a week's worth of healthy
meals to your home.

# 4

---

# Invest in

# Your Financial

# Health

---

Can you afford to live the life you really want? I don't mean having the means to buy a fancy car or a big home or to take an extravagant vacation. I'm talking about having the freedom to make decisions that will give you the quality of life you desire. Although most of us know by now that money doesn't bring happiness, the lack of money can bring plenty of pain. If you're living without financial reserves, it's impossible to be in control of your life. How can you leave a job that's making you crazy and affecting your health or take time off to care for a loved one? When will you take that trip you've been planning for the last ten years or start the business you've always dreamed of? It's impossible to "follow your bliss" when you've got a hefty mortgage to pay or feel saddled with unwanted debt.

A lack of financial reserves is the biggest obstacle to my clients, living the lives they most want. As we've already seen in chapter 1, money is just a piece of the larger puzzle called your life. The more trouble you have with money, however, the more energy this piece will take from you and the more challenging it will be to live the life you want. Extreme self-care includes taking care of your financial health. If you struggle to make ends meet, have trouble saving money, or feel burdened with unwanted debt, it's time to do something about it.

Ignorance is not bliss when it comes to your money. And don't be lulled by nonsense like "I'm too creative to understand those things" or "My husband/wife handles all that" or "I don't have enough to pay attention to," or, at the other end of the spectrum, "My broker/financial manager/banker knows it all." It's your money. It's your life.

In this chapter we'll examine the state of your financial health, an important ingredient to a high-quality life. I'll identify the common obstacles and the critical but often overlooked reason why abundance is illusory to many, and I'll provide you with the skills and support you'll need to regain your financial health. Once you know what to do and take action, you reclaim the power to live life on *your* terms!

Hundreds of books have been written about money—they run the gamut from "how to make smart investments" to "manifest abundance in thirty days." Very few, however, combine basic money management skills with the more emotional and even spiritual changes necessary to create a healthy, prosperous relationship with money. These necessary actions, when taken, will help you to trust your ability to handle more, the key to creating abundance.

Let's start by giving you a Financial Health Checkup. As you review the following list, check the items that apply to you and notice how you feel. When in doubt, consult your Wise Self for the truth.

*Financial Health Checkup* _____ *(Enter today's date)*
    _____ I balance my bank statement every month.
    _____ I always pay my bills on time.
    _____ I live debt free or utilize a plan to get there.
    _____ I contribute to a savings plan consistently.

_____ I don't dream about or depend on the lottery or other gimmicks to fund my financial future.

_____ I know where my money goes and how much I spend on personal and/or business expenses.

_____ I have a long-term financial plan that supports my present and future goals.

_____ I live well within my means.

_____ I am financially secure. I don't worry about money.

_____ I always carry enough cash with me.

_____ When I feel financially full, I share my wealth with others.

_____ I pay my credit cards in full each month.

_____ I pay my taxes on time.

_____ I have an excellent financial planner/accountant who supports my financial goals.

_____ I have a bookkeeping system that allows me to access my financial information at any moment.

How did you do? If this checklist feels overwhelming or depressing, don't worry. Eighty percent of the people that first take this test score between 3 and 6 points out of the possible 15. Becoming aware of the missing pieces in your financial puzzle is the first step. Once you know how to improve your financial health you can take one simple action and be on the road to fiscal fitness. Inaction is what keeps you a victim to external forces.

Most of us have never received any basic training in the art of handling money. It seems we go straight from independent, carefree childhood to the fiscal responsibilities of adulthood. Feeling insecure about money, we rarely seek help until we find ourselves in debt, approaching middle age and struggling to save, or coming up short at the end of the month. The way we handle money may be based on the way our parents handled money, and chances are they didn't receive any training either.

This lack of skill, discipline, and basic money management expertise gets you into trouble in several ways. First, there are concrete issues of debt and liability, what I call the practical issues. Following close behind are the emotional issues—a looming sense of anxiety about where your money goes and a sense of hopelessness about your ability to improve your financial state. Finally, you end up feeling frustrated, irresponsible, and bad about yourself, and this is what blocks you from increasing your wealth.

In my experience of working with thousands of people on money issues over the last fifteen years, I am convinced that the secret to creating the abundance you desire is very simple: once you take full responsibility for your financial health, money stops being a source of frustration and starts to flow into your life naturally.

If you are someone who never balances your checkbook, pays your bills late, or puts off filing your tax returns, then how will you trust yourself to handle more? Each time you neglect to handle your finances in a responsible way, you send a direct message to your Wise Self that you are not a good candidate for more. And, since your Wise Self is the part of you that is always concerned with your best interest, it's as if you hold yourself back from having more money until you prove to yourself that you can handle it.

To allow more abundance into your life, you must invest in your financial health. By shifting your attitude and developing "adult" money skills, you'll open to the abundance that is rightfully yours. Time and again I've watched as clients balance their checkbooks, start paying off debt, or ask for a well-deserved raise and thus open the door for more money to enter into their lives. My client Mary's story will help to further explain my point.

Mary is a successful sales associate who wants to make more money. She loves her job and has worked hard to take full advantage of her company's incentive program, but her monthly bonus checks have consistently stayed at $500 per month over the last year. Mary had read several books on creating money and was working hard to "think abundantly," but she felt frustrated with the results—nothing changed. After spending so much time and energy, Mary was ready to give up.

As I examined Mary's financial health, I learned that she had accumulated over $7,000 in credit card debt during the last three years. Her savings account balance of $2,000 fluctuated with her spending habits, often dipping below $500. And she usually paid her bills late, incurring interest charges and late fees. When I asked Mary how much her monthly living expenses were, she didn't know. This is not unusual—most people don't have an accurate account of what it costs them to live each month or where their money goes.

Her current financial situation provided important clues as to why Mary couldn't get beyond the $500-a-month mark. Without handling her finances better, Mary consistently sent a message to her Wise Self that she was not a good candidate for more. I explained that she was actually sabotaging her financial future by not taking responsible actions now. Once she understood that she might be keeping any additional income at bay, her anxiety decreased and she felt empowered to turn the situation around.

The path to financial freedom can be long and challenging. The commitment to become responsible with money is the key that opens the flood gates to more. Mary agreed to test my theory and began by making a list of her income and expenses to determine where her money went each month. Once she had a clear picture of her financial situation, she agreed to pay her bills on time.

Next came a plan to repay her charge card debt. The first action she took was the toughest, and it was a test of her commitment to becoming trustworthy with money. I asked her to cut the credit cards or promise to stop using them until she turned things around and could use them responsibly. Mary decided to give her cards to a trusted family member to hold for six months.

Over the next year, as Mary followed a step-by-step plan to improve her financial health, her bonus went from $500 to $1,500 a month. Almost like magic, it seemed that new customers appeared and her sales increased. But Mary knew better. The increase in her income was a direct result of the investment she made in her financial health. She (and her Wise Self) now knew she could handle more.

Restoring your financial health begins with a shift in attitude, from "dealing with money is too much work or too stressful" to "I'll do whatever it takes to restore my financial health." This shift sets the stage for action. When you take the necessary actions to get on track, you end up feeling good about yourself, and that's the key ingredient to creating abundance. When you feel secure about the way you handle money, you naturally attract more.

What's your attitude toward managing your money? Do you avoid thinking about it, expecting money to just take care of itself? Or do you obsess over every penny, trying to gain control over your worry and anxiety? When I ask clients and workshop participants what they think about money, I hear the following responses:

*I don't worry about money. I always have enough to get by.*
*I'm just not interested in learning how to manage my money well.*
*One of these days I'll figure out where my money goes.*
*The way I handle money determines the level of my personal success.*
*No one is ever really debt free. Having debt is just a way of life.*
*It costs too much to live these days. I'll never get ahead.*
*Money is a tool I use wisely to do what I want in my life.*
*I'm too young to worry about my financial future.*
*To have "real" money, you have to be born into a wealthy family.*

These attitudes reveal the kind of relationship you have with money. If your attitude is positive and proactive, you probably manage your money well and reap the benefits of feeling secure and empowered to make the choices you want in your life. If, on the other hand, your attitude is negative or nonchalant, you probably struggle with not having enough and end up feeling like a victim to external forces.

## Denial and Avoidance

Most people avoid dealing with money issues until there is a problem. They neglect to balance their checking account until the overdraft notices show up in the mail. Or they continue to spend money and put off saving until they hit middle age and realize the consequences. I know it seems easier to overlook or deny the nagging voice that reminds you to get a bookkeeping system in place or start paying off your debt, but eventually denial and inaction catch up with you. By ignoring the problem, you raise your threshold for pain and make it easier to put up with more. Mounting debt, a tarnished credit report, or an experience like my client Brian had are some of the consequences of ignoring your financial health.

During the holidays, Brian patiently waited in line at a sporting goods store, ready to purchase a Christmas gift for his brother. When it came his turn to pay, Brian pulled out his credit card and handed it to the cashier. After several attempts to get the card approved and a long, drawn-out call to the bank, the cashier informed him that he had reached his limit and his request had been denied.

Brian had sent in the minimum payment due each month but ignored the mounting balance. By the time he was refused credit, he had accumulated more than $5,000 worth of charge card debt and had gone over his limit. Although Brian knew he was getting close, he kept charging anyway. But the embarrassment of being turned down forced him out of his denial and made him confront the situation. Brian was caught in an endless loop of spending. The more he spent, the worse he felt and the more he denied the truth. This is one of the reasons why we may avoid taking action. Other reasons include the following.

I DON'T KNOW WHAT TO DO OR HOW TO DO IT. Not knowing how to balance a checkbook, set up a bookkeeping system, or invest money well is another obstacle that may be stopping you from taking action to improve your fiscal health. Without the "how to" knowledge, it's easy to just let your finances go. But getting the information and support you need to manage your money well can pay big dividends. Asking for help is a key to financial success. When my client Susan learned that a friend had earned over 25 percent on an investment fund she had started earlier in the year, she felt motivated to act. She found a good financial planner, made an appointment, and moved her money from the bank to a more lucrative investment vehicle that yielded her significantly higher returns. Susan realized that her lack of knowledge was actually costing her money.

**I'VE NEVER BEEN GOOD AT HANDLING MONEY.** Although you may desire to improve the ways you handle money, your past methods of handling money may prevent you from taking action now. Shame, fear, or guilt related to past behaviors (late payments resulting in collection procedures or defaults on a loan) can be paralyzing even when you've outgrown those old behaviors. As you replace your old financial habits with new ones, you'll start to feel better about yourself and your ability to take good care of your financial health.

My client Joanne was a successful business owner whose company was experiencing a high growth phase. She was having cash flow problems and needed a line of credit to manage the growth. But Joanne couldn't apply for the loan. She was paralyzed with fear that her credit report would prevent her from getting approved. Six years earlier, she had made some bad financial choices that caused debt to be charged off. Filled with regret, Joanne paid the price with the mark it had left on her credit report.

Joanne's shame from that past experience was affecting her present behavior. Her inability to apply for the loan was clouded by her belief that she was still that "bad, irresponsible person" and that others would view her that way. She neglected to acknowledge that she had changed considerably since that time and had become a much stronger credit risk.

Joanne and I walked step by step through the process of ordering her credit report, correcting any errors, and offering explanations about past credit problems. She was approved for financing and used this experience to upgrade her view of herself in relation to money. By taking action to remedy the situation in spite of her feelings, she experienced an immediate shift in her attitude and said good-bye to her past financial history.

**SOMEDAY I'LL HIT IT BIG.** For those of you who buy lottery tickets, order the "get rich quick" tapes late at night, or spend lots of time scheming to win the Publisher's Clearing House sweep-stakes, I have bad news: you're living in the future and letting the opportunity for real control over your financial present pass you by.

It's easy to be seduced by what could be. Many clients have spent money on a "guaranteed deal" only to have the deal fall through and find themselves left with debt. Remember, it all comes back to how responsible you are and the messages you send to your Wise Self about your ability to handle money.

Chasing the latest and greatest money-making opportunities, as my client Simon did, feeds denial and gets expensive, in terms of both time and money. Whether he was involved in several multilevel marketing companies or working on a potential "big" client, Simon constantly lived in the future, planning and spending for the life he would have once the money came through. He continued to accu-mulate debt and ignored the collection notices, convinced that he'd be able to pay it off soon. Eventually, Simon's future life caught up with him. He ran out of time and money and was forced to file for bankruptcy.

Don't be seduced! A sound financial plan is the only guarantee for a sound financial future.

---

If you're tired of worrying about money, fed up with feeling trapped and unable to make the choices you want, and ready to be free to live life on your terms, review the following Prescription for Financial Health and get to work! Action ignites the magic of more money. Send a strong message to your Wise Self that you're willing to do the inner and outer work necessary to become trustworthy with abun-dance. As you put these steps into action, you'll be rewarded in several ways. Your anxiety will lessen (almost immediately), you'll attract more money (sometimes in unexpected ways), and, most im-portant, you'll begin to feel good about yourself. Don't shut this book, avoiding action any longer. Get started now!

## RESTORE YOUR FINANCIAL HEALTH

Financial health is restored in two ways—first by doing the inner work of changing how you think and feel about money and then by doing the outer work of practical money management. While doing the inner work of shifting your beliefs, make sure you're taking the practical steps to improve your finances at the same time. Each requires action on your part, and these actions translate into more abundance.

Choose the actions that best fit your needs at this moment. If you haven't a clue as to why there is never enough money at the end of the month, go to the "Know Where Your Money Goes" section and get to work. If your accounts are balanced and the bills are paid but you can't seem to save consistently, check out the section entitled "Start Saving" or "Get Comfortable with More." Wherever you begin, take action right away!

### Prescription for Financial Health
#### The Inner Work—Change How You Think and Feel About Money

> Change your beliefs.
> Develop an attitude of gratitude.
> Share your wealth.
> Get comfortable with more.
> Respect yourself.

#### The Outer Work—Develop New Money Skills

> Ask for help.
> Balance your accounts.
> Know where your money goes.
> Cut your expenses.
> Pay your bills on time.
> Eliminate debt.

> *Repair your credit report.*
> *Start saving.*
> *Put a bookkeeping system in place.*
> *Create a personal spending plan.*
> *Invest in your future, invest in you.*

## THE INNER WORK—CHANGE HOW YOU THINK AND FEEL ABOUT MONEY

### Take Action! Change Your Beliefs

The thoughts and beliefs that you hold about money play an integral role in your financial health. If you constantly worry about how you'll pay your bills or eliminate your debt, these thoughts will contribute to the poor state of your financial health. Thoughts have power, and poor thoughts create poor results.

I'm not suggesting that you simply "think abundant thoughts" and let the problems take care of themselves—that's only solving half the problem. Instead, when you find yourself believing that your money problems will never get better, the quickest way to turn that belief around is to take a practical action. Choose a step from "The Outer Work" section that you know you need to take, and do it! Taking this action can immediately shift a negative belief, such as "my financial situation will never improve," to a more positive belief, like "things are getting better all the time."

Pay attention to how you think about money, and notice the beliefs that may be hidden beneath those thoughts. Sometimes we stumble onto our subconscious beliefs when we least expect it. My client Kate remembered a time when she discovered an interesting belief she held about wealth. While waiting at an intersection, she noticed a woman in a Jaguar who had pulled up next to her. As she looked over, her first thought was, "Gee, her husband must be very successful." Prompted by our discussions of how her thoughts might reveal her beliefs, Kate realized that she held a belief that women didn't become wealthy on their own. She was both surprised and embarrassed by this discovery. If she attributed that kind of wealth only to men, how could she expect to share in it herself?

What thoughts or beliefs do you hold about money? Do you still believe that money comes only as a result of hard work or that the desire for lots of money is not very spiritual? To uncover your hidden beliefs and further explore how you think and feel about money, finish the following statements:

*Money is*

_____

*My bank account is*

_____

*Those who have more money than me are*

_____

*Money never*

_____

*Money always*

_____

*When it comes to debt, I believe*

_____

*When I am faced with money problems, I believe*

_____

*When it comes to money management, I am*

_____

*For me to make more money, I must*

_____

*If I make too much money, then*

_____

*I can't make a lot of money because*

_____

*I deserve*

_____

What have you learned about yourself? The thoughts you hold about money have tremendous power, and the more responsible and abundant these thoughts are, the better. Start replacing your old beliefs by using the following examples to help turn them into more positive, wealth-enhancing ones:

> *From:* *I must work hard to make a lot of money.*
> *To:* *I make money by working smart.*
> *From:* *I always have just enough to get by.*
> *To:* *I always have more than enough.*
> *From:* *I can never really be debt free.*
> *To:* *I enjoy the freedom of living debt free.*
> *From:* *If I make too much money, people will want some.*
> *To:* *Abundance is my birthright, and I decide who gets it.*
> *From:* *I can't be spiritual and have lots of money.*
> *To:* *God wants me to be rich.*

Write your new beliefs on 3″-×-5″cards and place them on your bathroom mirror, near your bed, or on the dashboard of your car. This will help to install the new belief into your subconscious. Remember, though, affirmations do not take the place of practical action—affirmations *and* action ensure your financial success!

### *Take Action! Develop an Attitude of Gratitude*

A grateful state of mind is like a magnet. It radiates outward, sending a powerful force into the Universe to draw more abundance and joy toward you. Each day, plenty of signs show that the world is filled with lots to be grateful for. A sunny day, a gorgeous sunset, a car that stops to let you into traffic, or the perfect words of advice from an unexpected encounter are subtle examples of the endless supply of abundance available to us all.

One way to raise your thoughts and beliefs to a higher, more wealth-filled state is to notice where your life is already abundant, and be grateful. For example, when has something you've wanted or needed seemed to appear effortlessly? Have you ever found in your mailbox a piece of information you'd been thinking about that same day? Or received as a gift an item that you'd been eyeing for some time? These events are gentle reminders that wealth and abundance is the natural state of the Universe.

I remember one afternoon in early spring when the lilacs were in bloom. Lilacs are one of my favorite flowers, and I had wanted to pick some during the day but hadn't had a chance. Later that evening my in-laws came to visit. Imagine my surprise when I opened the door and found a vase filled with lilacs in my mother-in-law's hands. I instantly felt the abundance of the Universe in my life. To create a more grateful state of mind, try the following exercises:

1. Hang a big sheet of paper on a wall in your home and keep a set of colored markers nearby. Each time you pass by, write down one thing you feel grateful for. If you live with others, encourage them to add to the list as well. Make it a family gratitude list. Before you know it, the sheet will be filled with plenty of reminders of all there is to be grateful for, and you'll have trained your mind to notice the abundance that exists all around you.

2. Create a gratitude ritual. Use a regular event as a reminder to take note of the things you feel grateful for. For example, one of my clients keeps an ongoing gratitude list in his checkbook. Each month when he balances his accounts, he adds five items to the list. Not only does it remind him to stop and notice those things that he's grateful for, but it gives him an opportunity to look back over the list each month and remember the incredible abundance of his past.

3. Hold a gratitude celebration. Invite friends to a potluck dinner and ask them to bring a list of ten things that they feel grateful for. Throughout the evening, take turns sharing your list. You're bound to get more examples of things you can be grateful for too!

### Take Action! Share Your Wealth

Giving to others is a sure way to increase the flow of abundance in your life. Several years ago, I trained myself to stop worrying about money by giving some away as soon as I started to feel nervous about how much I had. I simply wrote a check to my favorite charity the moment I felt any concern. Sometimes those checks were as little as $5, but it reminded me to trust in a divine process and the cyclical nature of giving and receiving. As I watched money flow back into my life, it reinforced my belief that the world was an abundant place.

Be sure you're on the path to financial health before giving too much money away. Start small, and as you fill up your accounts you'll naturally want to share more. If you're not able to give away money, you can share your wealth in plenty of other ways. Get in the habit of practicing one of these ways every month. Other ways to share your wealth include the following:

- Bring leftover food to a local soup kitchen.
- Pick wildflowers and bring them to a local nursing home.
- Lend an ear to a friend in need.
- Offer your expertise to others (computer skills, organizing, etc.).
- Clean out your closets and donate the clothes you no longer wear.
- Hold the hand of a friend who's going to the hospital.

### Take Action! Get Comfortable with More

How do you feel about the prospect of having more money? Does the thought of added responsibility make you feel uncomfortable, excited, or overwhelmed? When you stop and consider your internal reactions to having more money, you can uncover potential blocks to attracting more. To help identify these blocks, take out your journal and make two columns. Title the first column "The benefits of having more money" and the second column "The drawbacks to having more money." Now take some time to consider both, and write down everything that comes to mind. What might you be afraid of or concerned about?

One way to uncover any subconscious beliefs you may hold about having more is to check in with how you feel about others who have more money than you. Do you hold any negative beliefs about those more fortunate? How did your family feel about people with money as you were growing up? Were family members critical of those more fortunate than they? If so, you may fear falling victim to the same judgments or criticisms. To get comfortable with an increase in your wealth, turn the drawbacks into benefits. For example, start blessing the good fortune of others. By removing your judgments against others, you'll remove the judgments you hold against yourself and free yourself to have more.

## Take Action! Respect Yourself

What you never ask for, you never get. Once you're committed to financial health and take the actions to prove it, you'll feel stronger about requesting the abundance that is yours. Extreme self-care means asking for a well-deserved raise, collecting money that's owed to you, or increasing your fees for the services you provide. For most people, asking for money is a challenging task. But with support and a plan, you can raise your level of self-respect and make it easier to ask for what's rightfully yours.

My client Dianna was an attorney with a private practice in a small town in the Midwest. She had several clients who owed her money, and although they ignored her invoices, Dianna felt uncomfortable calling to ask for payment. To claim the money that belonged to her, she needed to respect herself more.

As a start, Dianna implemented a 50 percent retainer policy for all new business, requiring a deposit before she began any work. Next, she made sure that her billing went out on time so her clients knew that she took her value seriously. Dianna also hired a bookkeeper to upgrade her financial systems and produce monthly reports that showed how the business was doing. This made Dianna feel more professional and in charge of the business.

By raising her standards and getting her own financial house in order, Dianna increased her level of confidence and self-respect. Feeling much better about herself, she found it easier to call each client to arrange a repayment plan. With the right language and a direct approach, Dianna's actions yielded the collection of 75 percent of her debt within sixty days. When she asked for what she deserved, others began to respect her too!

To help you ask for the money you deserve, try using a variation of the following statements:

### For money owed to you by others:

"John, I'm calling to speak with you about the $1,000 you owe my company. I'd like to work together to reach an agreement about how you'll pay that back. Let's start with your ideas. What plan would work best for you?"

Or

"Mary, I'm calling about your overdue account. It's been four months since we've received a check, and I'd like to get this cleared up as soon as possible. Is there a problem I should know about? Why don't you explain your current situation to me, and we'll see what we can work out together?"

### When asking for a raise:

"Karen, I'd like to speak with you about increasing my salary. It's been eighteen months since my last review, and a lot has changed. I'd like to sit down, get your feedback, review my accomplishments, and discuss appropriate compensation. When would be the best time to do that?"

*For increasing fees:*

> "Joseph, I'd like to let you know that I'll be increasing my
> fees as of January 1st. Instead of $_____per hour, I'll now
> be charging $_____. I wanted to give you enough notice
> to prepare. May I answer any questions?"

You'll notice that the tone of these examples is positive and
straightforward. When you have respect for yourself and your value,
you'll ask for what's yours with a gracious tone. Always approach
conversations about money with the intention of partnership. If
you're dealing with someone who owes you money and does not
intend to repay you, then save yourself the emotional struggle and
have an attorney or collection agency handle it. Honor your self-care
first—don't get hooked into emotional battles disguised as financial
ones. I've provided resources at the end of this chapter for situations
that require professional support.

––––––

Now let's look at the outer work—the practical, day-to-day money
management skills needed to take good care of your financial health.

## THE OUTER WORK—DEVELOP NEW MONEY SKILLS

### Take Action! Ask for Help

In our culture, it's still a social taboo to talk about money. Financial
problems are kept secret, even among family members. Yet you can
feel tremendous relief and freedom in sharing your concerns and
questions about money with safe people. Whether it's from friends
and family or a professional accountant, bookkeeper, or financial
planner, we all need support in learning new financial skills.

Although I was a tax consultant for many years, I do not prepare
my own taxes anymore. I wouldn't touch them. Our tax laws are

complicated and always changing, and the effort to keep up is more than I have time for. So I get help. I want an objective, well-trained professional to bounce ideas off of and to provide the tax planning and preparation that are key to the success of my financial future.

Asking for help is the number one solution to the obstacle of denial and avoidance. Finding the help you need will always make taking action much easier. It's important that the people with whom you choose to work are well suited to your personality. Too often I've seen clients give their power away to someone with whom they don't feel comfortable simply because the individual is more knowledgeable about money. You want a partnership, a positive working relationship with someone who respects you and your financial concerns. The more fear you have, the more sensitive support you'll need, so when you find yourself not knowing what to do or having trouble moving forward, ask for help.

Engage in a dialogue about money with your coaching partner or group. It's comforting to learn that others share similar fears and concerns. This is one area where having support from others can mean the difference between financial success and failure. Begin a dialogue about money by answering the following questions. If you're not using the support of a partner or group, then use your journal to write about your experiences.

> *What did your family teach you about money? How did they*
> *    influence your beliefs?*
> *What has been your deepest wound regarding money?*
> *What financial success are you most proud of?*
> *What is your biggest secret about money?*
> *What are your financial dreams?*

Finish the dialogue by having each person complete the following sentence:

> *When it comes to money, I need help with*

_____

Then, arrange to get this help. Give each other the support you need, or find a professional to help. When interviewing professionals, be sure and ask yourself the following questions:

*Does this person have experience with situations like mine?*
*Does this person seem to enjoy what he or she does?*
*Is it easy to talk to her?*
*Does she treat me with respect?*
*How available is he to answer questions?*
*Can I easily afford his fee?*
*Do I feel safe and relaxed with this person?*
*Have I asked for at least three references?*

### Take Action! Balance Your Accounts

Balancing your accounts is an important step in reclaiming your financial power. When you let your checkbook go and rely on a "good idea" of where it stands, it's usually a setup for more lax behavior later on. If you can't get it balanced yourself, either hire someone else to do it or stop using the account long enough to let all checks clear. Then get a true balance from the bank. If you're not sure how to balance your own checkbook, you can do the following:

1. Use the step-by-step "How to balance your checkbook" worksheet on the back of your bank statement.
2. Visit a local branch of your financial institution and have one of the assistants show you how.
3. Use a computer-based software program (like Quicken) to balance the accounts.

With the growing use of ATM machines, it's more challenging to balance bank statements manually. But getting your accounts balanced is an important part of the process. The more you know about your financial situation, the more you'll add to your personal sense of security and financial well-being and feel motivated to continue on the road to improving your financial health.

My client Samuel never considered himself a "numbers person." He never bothered to read his monthly bank statements. Instead, when he needed to know his balance, he simply called the bank for a "ballpark" idea of how much money he had. Samuel said he "didn't have the patience to figure out my bank statement" and decided these simple check-in calls would be easier. But Samuel lived in a constant state of anxiety about money. He never felt financially secure, and at the age of forty-three he had very little savings set aside. When I suggested that this one small action could have a large impact on his mental well-being, as well as his financial well-being, he reluctantly agreed to give balancing his account a try.

Samuel called a friend (who happened to work for a local bank) and asked for help. His friend guided him through a step-by-step process, and Samuel was surprised by how easy it was. Once his account was accurate and up to date, he felt an overwhelming sense of accomplishment and pride. Samuel marked this step as the beginning of a whole new relationship with money.

Remember, one simple act is all it takes to turn your financial situation around.

### Take Action! Know Where Your Money Goes

Ignorance is not bliss when it comes to money. Don't put off any longer getting an accurate account of where your money goes. Instead of documenting every penny (which feels like a daunting and unrealistic task to most people), start by creating a simple map of your financial picture. Make a list of your income and expenses for one month by filling in the appropriate information below:

> **Total monthly income:** _____
> **Monthly expenses:**
>     *Rent/mortgage*
>     *Utilities*

*Insurance*
*Food*
*Clothing*
*Entertainment*
*Loan payments*
*Cash expenditures*
*Other*
**Money left over:** _____
**Amount to go into savings:** _____

Are you earning enough money to cover your expenses and save consistently? Is there money left over after expenses? Do you know where your cash goes? If the answer is "I'm not sure," then do yourself a favor and keep a more detailed account of your expenses for one month. Set up a system whereby you jot down the amount of money spent at the end of the day before you go to bed. Your journal is a great place for this information.

At the end of one month, total your expenses and subtract that amount from your income to find out how profitable you really are (income − expenses = profit). When it comes to money, the numbers don't lie. Knowing where your money goes is an important step in changing your spending and saving habits. The actual numbers always reveal the truth about the state of your financial health, so be prepared!

When my client Madeline mapped out her finances, she understood why there was never enough money at the end of the month. By using her charge card for most purchases, she consistently spent more than she earned. Seeing her finances in black and white made it clear why she felt stressed about money all the time. It was time to cut back and create a smart financial plan.

## Take Action! Cut Your Expenses
As you review where your money is spent each month, identify the expenses that are unnecessary, and eliminate them. Ask yourself

which ones really add value to your life. Aside from the necessities like food, shelter, clothing, and heat, do the other expenses make sense? Do you really enjoy all the times you go out to eat? Do you buy clothes that sit in your closet? To improve your financial health, you may need to be willing to change your lifestyle.

When Thomas Stanley and William Danko interviewed millionaires for their bestselling book *The Millionaire Next Door,* they discovered a common strategy that contributed to their wealth—most lived below their means. If you have trouble deciding which expenses to eliminate, you can ask someone you trust to look over your expenses and offer creative ways to reduce it. Or imagine that half your income was suddenly taken away, and then decide how you'd cut expenses.

For a while, you may need to cut back on things that you really enjoy, like eating out or buying new clothes or gifts. But this teaches you to want something without having it right away—an important skill to develop if you want to achieve financial freedom. Delayed gratification is an important muscle to build. Giving up something you really want for the sake of your financial health sends a very strong message to your Wise Self that you are trustworthy with more.

When my client Fred, a psychotherapist whose practice was suffering because of managed care, decided to cut back his expenses, he gave up going to baseball games for the remainder of the season. Although he loved the time spent with his friends, the games were costing him money he didn't have. Not surprisingly, over the next six months Fred added seven new clients to his practice, reduced his debt by 15 percent, and added $350 to his savings account.

Living well does not require you to spend a lot of money. And living within your means does not mean giving up those things that bring you joy. It's all a matter of personal taste. You might choose to live a slower-paced lifestyle, working and earning less, yet include a weekly massage as a mandatory expense. Or you might decide to give up going out to lunch every day during the week for the experience of eating dinner one night at a fine restaurant. The key is to stop and ask yourself what expenses truly make you happy. Go for the quality of experience, not the quantity or short-term fix. Having afternoon tea at the Four Seasons may be the perfect way to celebrate a special occasion, instead of having an elaborate party or expensive dinner.

Often the most enjoyable experiences cost little or no money at all. Sharing a home-cooked meal with good friends who make us laugh, enjoying time with our children or parents, and taking a long walk on the beach are the kinds of experiences that enrich our lives and make great memories. Incorporate more of these experiences into your daily life, and you'll find it much easier to let go of expenses that are often short-lived. Take a moment to think about the experiences that have cost little or no money at all yet brought you joy. List five examples here:

1. _____
2. _____
3. _____
4. _____
5. _____

Examples from clients include these:

| | |
|---|---|
| *Having a picnic lunch at the beach* | *Making love* |
| *Spending time with friends* | *Taking a long, hot bath* |
| *Reading a good book* | *Taking an evening walk with a loved one* |
| *Watching old movies* | *Flying a kite with a child* |

Now look back over your expenses and replace the "empty" ones with examples from your list.

## Take Action! Pay Your Bills on Time

When you are extended credit or services prior to payment, someone is trusting you to keep your word. How you feel about yourself makes all the difference. When you're consistently late in paying your bills, it affects how you feel about yourself, whether you realize it or not. On some level, knowing that you're "out of integrity" stops the flow of abundance. I've yet to meet anyone who felt good about not keeping promises.

During a coaching session, my client Pat and I were reviewing her week when she relayed a story that demonstrates my point. Pat was strolling through her local mall when she spotted the owner of a flower shop to whom she owed money. Realizing that she had once again failed to pay the past-due bill, she quickly turned and went in a different direction. Later that day, Pat was in a bad mood. It wasn't until she got into bed that evening that she made the connection between her mood and the experience earlier in the day.

Paying your bills late is expensive. It costs you more than late charges and added interest—it may cost you your reputation with others and, more important, with yourself. To make bill paying easier, you can do the following:

1. Coordinate the dates of when bills are due. Most companies are happy to do this, and it will make it easier to pay all your bills at the same time each month.
2. Use electronic home banking. More banks are starting to offer computerized, home-banking services. The technology is very user friendly, and with the push of a button you can pay bills automatically each month.
3. Hire a bookkeeper to pay your bills. If you're too busy to pay your bills on time, spend the $25–$50 per month that it will probably cost to get it handled. Let someone else worry about paying them on time.

### Take Action! Eliminate Debt

Make a commitment to pay off old debt. If your bills are overdue, communicate with all creditors and explain your situation. Telling the truth about your financial hardship honors your integrity and lets your creditors know that you take your responsibility seriously.

Create a debt repayment plan using the following guidelines:

1. Make a list of all outstanding debt.
2. Move the debt with the highest interest rates to the top of the list.
3. Focus on paying off the high-interest loans and charge cards first.
4. Make the minimum payments on the rest.
5. When you've paid one debt in full, cross it off the list.
6. Reward yourself with an *inexpensive* celebration.

If you're overwhelmed with debt, ask for help. Credit counseling services are available that may be able to help you get interest rates reduced or eliminated altogether. For help with credit problems, you can contact the following groups:

Consumer Credit Counseling Services. (800) 873–2227
www.powersource.com/cccs

Money Management by Mail. (800) 762–2271
www.moneymanagementbymail.com

Both organizations provide helpful, free services for those who have debt problems.

Paying off old debt involves more than just eliminating costs. Old debt holds old energy. The cost of dinner with an old girlfriend or a medical bill from a past illness remains on your charge card balance. This debt holds the energy of that experience, and paying it off is essential to moving on with your life.

I've watched as a Divine presence rallies to support clients in unexpected ways when they make a commitment to pay off their debt. My client Carl had $15,000 in old debt that was dragging him down. He was tired of carrying the extra weight and made a commitment to spend the next year doing whatever it would take to get it paid off. He moved to a smaller apartment, cut his expenses by 50 percent, and took a second, part-time job. He decided to put all this extra income toward his debt. At the end of eight months Carl's debt was reduced to $8,500.

One month later, an elderly friend of the family whom Carl had helped out over the years passed away and left him $8,500 as a gift. With this, Carl paid the remainder of his debt. What brought Carl this good fortune? I believe it was his commitment to do whatever it took to eliminate his debt and his willingness to take consistent and sometimes difficult actions toward his goal of financial health.

A final note about debt—don't get pulled in by the offers of credit you receive in the mail or over the phone. Credit card sponsors send out 2.4 million separate offers for new cards each year *(Money* magazine, June 1997), and with lower rates, banks are forever pushing equity loans. There will always be a telemarketer offering you the latest and greatest charge card rates, especially as your credit improves. For them, it's money made easily, and the sales pitch never ends. But all you're left with is a pile of debt. Just say no!

### Take Action! Repair Your Credit Report

Earlier I mentioned Joanne, a client who had a difficult time applying for credit because of the condition of her credit report. Credit reports can cause a tremendous amount of shame for clients with poor past financial histories. Are you afraid to apply for a loan because your credit history may affect your ability to get approved? Most people never see what their credit report looks like. Don't wait until you need a loan to see what your credit report says about your financial history.

A credit report contains the following information:

*Identification information—name, date of birth, social security number*
*Address information—current and previous addresses*
*Employment information—current and past employers*
*Account information—creditors, payment history, balances, etc.*
*Public record information—tax liens, bankruptcy, collections, etc.*

This information is made available from three major credit bureaus in the United States to anyone considering extending you credit. The credit bureau does not determine whether you are a good credit risk—the lender does, based on the information it receives.

Order your credit report now. It's not uncommon for credit reports to have errors, so you'll want to be sure yours is an accurate depiction of your financial history. In the resource section at the end of this chapter, I've listed an easy way for you to receive your credit reports from the three major bureaus, as well as the best way to make any corrections.

Consider the inner work needed to repair your credit report as well. A credit report is not a reflection of you—only of your financial history. You may need to forgive yourself for past behaviors. And at times you may even need to repay an old debt that was charged off or included in bankruptcy proceedings in order to feel good about yourself. Do whatever it takes to complete the past and feel confident about yourself as a credit risk.

### Take Action! Start Saving

We've all heard the rule "pay yourself first," but it's tough to do when your income does not exceed your expenses. Profitability is the first priority. Once you've cut your expenses and have money left over, you need to start saving immediately. Save as much as you can, at as early an age as possible, and invest it well. When you combine the power of compound interest (earning money on both your initial investment and your earnings), with investing at an early age, it yields powerful results. For example, let's imagine that you set a goal of having $1,000,000 in the bank at age sixty-five. Let's see how much money you'd need to invest annually, earning 10 percent interest, based on when you begin.

If you decide to start saving at age twenty, you'd need to invest $1,391 per year to reach your goal. If, however, you decided to begin saving at age thirty, you would need to invest 3,690 per year. At age forty, your savings amount would need to be $10,168 per year. And finally, starting at age fifty, you would have to save a whopping

$31,474 per year in order to reach $1,000,000. As you can see, time is one of your strongest investment tools!

Now let's look at the power of compound interest from another perspective. Let's imagine that you've save $1,000 per year from age twenty until age thirty (a total principal investment of $10,000). If you received 10 percent interest on your investment, you'd now have $15,937 in total (an earning of $5,937 in interest). If you were to let this total amount sit in your savings account, continuing to earn 10 percent interest, without investing another dime of your money, by age sixty-five, you'd have a total of $447,869. That's a total of $437,869 in interest!

The point is to start saving now! Begin with a goal of saving at least 10 percent of your income before taxes. In other words, if your annual income is $40,000, put $4,000 away in some kind of investment vehicle. Break it down into monthly payments (e.g., $334) and include it as an expense. The older you are, the higher this percentage will need to be to reach the necessary financial reserves for retirement. Be sure to ask for help from a professional to determine the right amount for you.

If money is tight, begin with the simple act of saving change in a jar on your desk. This new habit will make it easier for you to save more as your profit increases. Develop a savings discipline. Think of it as a spiritual discipline, an investment in you and your Wise Self. After all, putting money away consistently is an act of extreme self-care and is essential to creating more wealth.


### Take Action! Put a Bookkeeping System in Place
Plenty of manual and computerized bookkeeping systems are available to help keep your finger on the pulse of your finances. Using a good system to maintain your financial records keeps them up to date and allows you to always know where you stand. If you're unsure about how to set it up, hire someone to help put the system in place. Don't procrastinate because you don't know what to do—let some-

one else do it. The time saved and money spent are well worth the cost of knowing where your money goes.

Like the shoemaker who never makes shoes for herself, I kept putting off improving my bookkeeping system, feeling overwhelmed by the task. Yet for two years I knew that my personal and business financial information needed to be organized, by putting it on Quicken (my favorite financial software package). During a session with my own coach, she challenged me to have it completed by the following week. She had heard me complain long enough and reminded me to put my own beliefs to the test. I decided to see how this undone task might be affecting my income.

Three days later, I spent twelve straight hours putting every account I had onto Quicken. Once this was completed, it felt like a tremendous weight had been lifted from my shoulders. When it came time to do my taxes, not only did the preparation time take me two hours instead of two days, but my income for the year had increased by 35 percent. On some level I'm convinced that I had been holding my income back by not completing this project.

Don't hold your income back any longer. Use the resources at the end of this chapter to help you put a bookkeeping system in place now.

### Take Action! Create a Personal Spending Plan

Develop a formula that allows you to feel good about how you spend your money—a personal spending plan. I no longer ask my clients to create budgets. In fact, I try never to use the word "budget" anymore. Negative feelings like guilt, deprivation, and restriction associated with the word make it unlikely that clients will follow through in using one. Instead I take a much simpler approach.

Once you commit to a specific amount of money that you'll save each month and you've paid off all your debt (with the possible exception of a car loan or mortgage), then consider the amount remaining as your living expenses. In other words, when you've satisfied your savings goal each month, you spend what's left over on living. If you don't have it, you can't spend it.

### Take Action! Invest in Your Future, Invest in You!

Take courses, read books, hire a coach—do anything that will educate you about money matters. Stay informed. Keep on top of the new software, tax breaks, and investment vehicles—all those tools that will help keep your financial health in good shape. And, if that feels overwhelming, make sure that you have a top-notch accountant who will keep you informed.

One of the easiest ways I keep informed about investment strategies is to listen to talk radio. I've learned a tremendous amount from two local financial planners who have a show called *The Money Experts*. They are funny, personable, and very bright. They make learning easy. When I travel by car at the appropriate time, I switch to their show and listen as they coach callers about everything from investing in mutual funds to refinancing mortgages or buying collectibles. Check to see if there is a money program in your area, and tune in.

Ask others about their profitable investments and find out how they did it. Get referrals from family and friends on books, courses, and financial planners. Remember, some people make it their life's work to study investment strategies. Interview candidates (see the "Ask for Help" section earlier in the chapter for questions to ask) and be sure to check references. The right professional will guide you on the path to your financial goals.

Investing in the future also means investing in you! While you're contributing to your savings plan, remember to allocate some of your income to training, updating your skills, and taking care of yourself, like updating your image or wardrobe. Investing in *you* means a stronger financial future as well.

My client Tim was so relieved that he had spent $1,000 on a computer training course the previous year. While all his friends thought he was crazy, he knew that the Internet would become an important tool in future business and that computer skills would be more in demand. He knew this would ensure his career advancement. While those same friends were playing catch-up a year later, Tim landed a high-paying job that gave him extra money to invest in savings. In the end, his investment in himself paid big dividends.

———

Going through the process of restoring your financial health and learning new skills is a long-term commitment. By doing both the inner and the outer work, you've set in place a strong foundation of new habits and beliefs that will secure your financial future. Go back to the Financial Health Checkup at the beginning of the chapter and update your list.

True security comes from much more than a fat bank account and no debt. It comes from having reserves in other areas as well—love, community, spiritual well-being, resources, and marketable skills, to name a few. But if money is in short supply, it affects every one of these areas.

Abundance is your birthright. You don't need to have all the steps completed to reap the rewards. Look for the signs that will remind you that you're on the right track—an unexpected financial gift, an increase in income, or an error in your checkbook that puts more money in your pocket. Whatever the case, expect a divine power to support your efforts—when you honor yourself, it always will.

COACHING REMINDERS
*Abundance flows when you trust yourself enough to handle it.*

- Action ignites the magic of more money.
- Restore your financial health:
    Do the inner work—change how you think and feel about money.
    Do the outer work—practice new money skills.

# RESOURCES

*BOOKS*

**The Nine Steps to Financial Freedom** by Suze Orman (New York: Crown Publications, 1997)
Suze Orman goes beyond the nuts and bolts of managing money to explore the psychological, even spiritual power money has in our lives.

**Your Money or Your Life: Transforming Your Relationship with Money and Achieving Financial Independence** by Joe Dominguez and Vicki Robin (New York: Penguin USA, 1993)
Joe Dominguez and Vicki Robin present their revolutionary, inspiring, and empowering nine-step program for transforming your relationship with money and achieving financial independence.

**Prospering Woman: A Complete Guide to Achieving the Full, Abundant Life** by Ruth Ross (San Rafael, Calif.: Whatever Publishing, 1982)
In her work as a therapist, Dr. Ross has found that the closer many women get to personal success, the more uncomfortable they become. Writing with empathy and encouragement, she shows women how to overcome this barrier to prosperity and how to turn their special strengths into powerful tools.

**Dynamic Laws of Prosperity** by Catherine Ponder (Marina del Rey, Calif.: Devorss & Company, 1984)
One of the all-time great books on manifestation. Have your journal ready to write down the affirmations contained throughout this book.

**The Seven Laws of Money** by Michael Phillips (Boston, Mass.: Shambhala, 1997)
These seven simple laws are the secret to a healthy, fearless attitude toward money, liberating its creative potential for everyone.

***How to Get Out of Debt, Stay Out of Debt and Live Prosperously*** by Jerrold
        Mundis (New York: Bantam, 1990)
This is an excellent resource by the founder of Debtors Anonymous. This
book offers the first essential, complete, effective guide to getting out of
debt once and for all.

***Spiritual Economics*** by Eric Butterworth (Unity Village, Mo.: Unity
        Books, 1993)
This book helps you to reshape your attitude about money, spirituality, and
personal prosperity.

***Creating Money*** by Sanaya Roman and Duane Packer (Tiburon, Calif.: H.J.
        Kramer, Inc., 1988)
A step-by-step spiritual guide to creating money and prosperity.

***Smart Questions to Ask Your Financial Advisers*** by Lynn Brenner and Mark
        Matcho (New York: Bloomberg Press, 1997)
This book gets right to the heart of successful financial planning with smart,
practical questions everyone needs to ask to assure themselves of getting the
best return on their money.

***The Millionaire Next Door: The Surprising Secrets of America's Wealthy*** by
        Thomas J. Stanley and William D. Danko (Marrena, Ga.: Long Street
        Press, 1996)
This book exposes how ordinary Americans get and stay rich without in-
heritance, advanced degrees, or lottery jackpots. Readers learn the seven
common denominators that show up again and again among people who
have built their personal fortunes from scratch.

***4 Easy Steps to Successful Investing*** by Jonathan D. Pond (New York: Avon,
        1997)
This informative companion book coincides with the PBS broadcast and
offers investment strategies for both the novice and the sophisticated
investor.

**10 Steps to Financial Success: A Beginner's Guide to Saving and Investing**
    by W. Patrick Naylor (New York: John Wiley & Sons, 1997)
This ten-step, easy-to-follow guide provides novice investors with an understanding of sound money management and investing techniques. Contains financial planning for anyone—even those who can spare only $25 a month.

**How to Retire Rich** by James O'Shaughnessy (New York: Broadway Books,
    1998)
Investment wizard James O'Shaughnessy offers valuable insight on everything from savings, to investing, to your 401(k), so that you can create the fully funded retirement plan you deserve.

**The Ultimate Credit Handbook** by Gerri Detweiler (New York: Plume,
    1997)
An excellent resource for improving your credit and reducing your debt.

## BANKRUPTCY

### The Bankruptcy and Financial Wellness Center
http://www.bk-info.com/mh2.htm
    This organization gives great information about when and why to consider bankruptcy and what to do next if you decide that it's the best decision for you.

### ABI World
http://www.abiworld.org/consumer/A.html
    The American Bankruptcy Institute's Consumer Information Center provides information about bankruptcy, its terminology, the filing process, and where to find local assistance.

**National Association of Consumer Bankruptcy Attorneys**

http://nacba.com

(703) 803–7040

NACBA is an organization of more than nine hundred attorneys across the country who primarily represent debtors in consumer bankruptcies. This Web site is intended for use by NACBA members and also to provide information regarding bankruptcy law to the general public.

*DEBT CONSOLIDATION*

**Debt Counselors of America**

http://www.dca.org

(800) 680–3328

An IRS-approved, nonprofit organization that assists families and individuals with debt, credit, money, and financial questions, problems, or difficulties.

**National Credit Counseling Services/Genus Credit Management**

http://www.nccs.org

(888) 793–4368

A nonprofit community service organization that provides a wide range of financial counseling services and educational programs for consumers to help financially distressed families and individuals more effectively manage their personal finances and credit.

**Credit Counseling Center of America**

http://www.cccamerica.org

(800) 493–2222

A nonprofit organization that provides free credit counseling for individuals or families who are having trouble making payments to credit cards, banks, and financial institutions.

## BOOKKEEPING SYSTEMS

### Quicken
http://www.quicken.com

### QuickBooks
http://www.intuit.com/quickbooks

### Peachtree
http://www.peachtree.com

### MYOB
http://www.myob.com

### One-Write Plus
(800) 649–1720 or (603) 880–5100 (manual and electronic)

## OTHER

### Payco American
Brookfield, WI
http://www.payco.com
(800) 826–4271

> Payco American Corporation (Payco), provides a full range of accounts receivable management services to credit-granting clients. Payco serves clients through a nationwide network of offices, including an office in Puerto Rico.

### Credit Bureau Systems
http://www.creditbureau.com
(800) 688–0048

> Provides support with collections, receivables management, skip tracing, etc.

## Check Free

http://www.checkfree.com/topics.html

(770) 441–3387

Provides information on bill payment software.

## CreditComm Services LLC

10400 Eaton Place, Suite 400

Fairfax, VA 22030

(800) 789–9952

For approximately $30, this organization will provide you with an easy-to-read report on your personal credit history from the three major bureaus in the United States. They also provide assistance for correcting inaccurate information and, for an additional fee, will monitor your credit files from all three bureaus throughout the year.

## Assist U

http://www.assistu.com

(410) 666–5900

Assist U makes referrals to virtual bookkeepers.

## Institute of Certified Financial Planners

http://www.icfp.org

(303) 759–4900

The Institute of Certified Financial Planners (ICFP) is a professional association with more than 12,000 CFP® licensees and candidate members nationwide.

## American Accounting Association

http://www.rutgers.edu/Accounting/raw/aaa/aaa.htm

(941) 921–7747

## American Institute of Certified Public Accountants

http://www.aicpa.org

# 5

## What's

## Fueling

## You?

The alarm went off at 7 A.M. Meredith stretched and began her morning routine. Giving herself time to wake slowly and start the day off right, she sat up in bed and pulled out her journal. Meredith often began her mornings by writing a few spontaneous pages and finishing with a time of prayer. When finished, she took a hot shower, packed her bag for the gym, and sat down to enjoy her breakfast. Meredith smiled as she gazed out her kitchen window at the sight of several small birds hovering around the bird feeder. Another beautiful sunny day was unfolding before her. She looked forward to exercising, sitting in the sauna afterward, and arriving at work refreshed and ready to meet her favorite client at 10 A.M.

Meredith is an account executive for an ad agency. Her friends and colleagues marvel at her ability to take such good care of herself while working in an industry that is notorious for competitive stress and crazy deadlines. But Meredith is smart. Her commitment to extreme self-care had already proven that she could get more done in a relaxed and focused way than in the typical frenzied pace that had most of her colleagues spinning their wheels. Instead of accepting that condition as a given in her field, she made a conscious choice to use a different kind of energy to get things done—she used premium fuel.

If you've begun to make the changes outlined in the previous chapters of this book, your life is in better shape, and you're ready to take a closer look at what gives you energy—the kinds of behaviors and habits that fuel you. As you learned in chapter 3, we all need energy to live day to day. Energy enables us to focus, take action consistently, and live our lives fully. But where do we get this energy? What fuels the body, mind, and spirit?

Various types of fuel give us the energy needed to take action. Some fuels are better than others. For example, energy that comes from exercise, nutritious food, and the love and support of great people fuels you and supports your long-term health in a positive way. Other energy sources such as adrenaline, caffeine, sugar, and anxiety may fuel you in intense bursts but ultimately put your health at risk. Like gasoline, you can choose fuel that's slow burning and lasts over time, or you can use fast-burning rocket fuel, the kind that gives you a powerful immediate boost but burns out quickly. Both types of energy can get certain jobs done, but only one supports your long-term physical, emotional, and spiritual health. One is premium, the other is junk fuel.

Meredith made a conscious decision to switch from junk fuel to premium. You can too. Unfortunately, many of us run on the less desirable fuel. Sam, who has an ongoing personality conflict with his boss, is fueled by fear. This fear causes him to feel stressed beyond measure and to work ridiculous hours trying to avoid confrontations. Judy, fueled by a need for approval, volunteers her time in too many places and ends up frantically working nights and weekends to get everything done. And Pauline, who drinks more than a pot of coffee throughout the day, uses caffeine to stay focused and awake. These types of energy sources—fear, anxiety, and external stimulants such as caffeine and sugar—are the kinds of fuel that put our long-term health at risk. They contribute to the most widely used fuel in America today—adrenaline.

## RUNNING ON ADRENALINE

Adrenaline seems to be the drug of choice among many new clients. It's easy to understand why. Advertising agencies spend billions of dollars raising our adrenaline levels by telling us to "act now before it's too late!" Television and radio bombard us with fast-action programming and powerful images (both good and bad) that raise our anxiety levels. And the onslaught of computers, hundreds of cable TV channels, and the Internet tempts us to tune in for the latest news and information twenty-four hours a day. All these things contribute to the overstimulation of our adrenal system, making it hard to slow down and relax.

Overuse of the adrenal system keeps your body programmed to stay "on alert." This state keeps the fight-or-flight system ready to respond and can eventually cause adrenal burnout. Dr. Glen Rothfeld, a holistic physician, has seen the results of adrenal burnout frequently. He says, "Adrenaline is used like a drug. [It] pushes our body to work faster and harder with the energy reserves we have. The end result can be a crash of blood sugar, of energy, and a depletion of our nutritional reserves." He goes on to state that "adrenaline junkies are looking for the boost that their fight-or-flight response gives them, but like other junkies, that boost gets less and less satisfying, even as it hooks them. High adrenaline levels over time can lead to heart disease, diabetes, and chronic fatigue states. They can also lead to chronic insomnia, suppressed immunity, and to anxiety and depression."

Adrenaline is produced by the adrenal gland, which regulates the body's fight-or-flight response to stimulating experiences. These experiences can be both positive and negative. When you're late for an appointment and you hit a traffic jam, the rush of anxiety you feel sitting in the car is adrenaline. When the deal you've been working on finally comes through, the excitement you feel also comes from adrenaline. Adrenaline isn't bad, but when we develop habits like constantly running late or juggling too many projects at once, it gets us into trouble.

An example of this overstimulated adrenaline response came from my client Alex, who always felt compelled to check his phone and e-mail messages. Although he didn't realize it, the reason Alex felt so compelled was that his anxiety level increased every time he checked his voice mail or e-mail. During the day when he felt a slump in his energy, he said that checking his messages "gave him a little boost." It had become a disturbing habit, since he was now checking them both eight or even ten times in one day. Even on vacation, he had to find a phone and check in. As a way to eliminate this anxious habit, I suggested that he limit it to twice a day, checking his messages at noon and again at four in the afternoon. At first this was difficult. Alex felt drawn to this distraction almost as though it was an addiction. I explained that, in fact, relying on anxiety and adrenaline can become addictive. I suggested that Alex get a drink of water or take a short walk every time he felt tempted to check again. Within a month, he had broken this habit and no longer felt compelled to constantly retrieve his messages.

The concept of adrenaline as an energy source is foreign to most clients. Rarely are they aware that they're using their fight-or-flight response as fuel. They become so accustomed to leading busy lives and rushing to get things done that they've developed certain habits and behaviors that create a vicious cycle of adrenaline overuse.

To test whether adrenaline might be fueling you, answer the following questions:

### Are You Running on Adrenaline?
_____ Do you consistently overcommit yourself personally and professionally?

_____ Do you double-book social engagements?

_____ Are you usually late for appointments?

_____ Do you repeatedly check your voice mail or e-mail throughout the day?

_____ Is your schedule so full that there's no time left for you?

_____ Do you feel lost without your beeper, cell phone, or laptop?

_____ Do you put things off to the last minute or use tight deadlines to get things done?

_____ Do you find yourself in frequent conflicts with others?

_____ Do you usually speed when driving?

_____ Does it seem like your car's fuel gauge is always on or near empty?

_____ Do you hate to stop and ask for or read directions?

_____ Do you live on the edge financially?

_____ Do you always feel pressed for time?

_____ Do you put off making decisions or taking action in spite of the anxiety it causes?

_____ Does the thought of being bored make you nervous and uncomfortable?

_____ If the phone rings as you're heading out the door, do you answer it anyway?

_____ Do you wake in the middle of the night with your thoughts racing, unable to sleep?

_____ Do you juggle several projects at once?

_____ Are you constantly coming up with new ideas to pursue?

_____ Do you often forget to follow through on commitments?

If you answered yes to five or more questions, you may be running on adrenaline. These behaviors generate the constant hum of anxiety, and this anxiety pumps adrenaline into your body. There are better ways to fuel yourself, but before we consider them, let's look at how to kick the adrenaline habit and start using premium fuel.

## KICK THE ADRENALINE HABIT

Running on adrenaline can be a tough habit to kick. It's one of the hardest changes to make, and yet I can assure you that on the other side of a life fueled by adrenaline is the peace of mind you long for. The challenge with kicking the adrenaline habit is that adrenaline can feel exhilarating and be easily mistaken as a good source of energy. For example, I've heard clients say things like: "I need tight deadlines to get things done, it motivates me," or "Filling my schedule keeps me pumped and on my toes." Adrenaline is sneaky, and its negative effects build up over time. Once you discover that you're being fueled by it, it's easier to see the changes that need to be made. And once you stop running on adrenaline, other healthy choices, like eating well and exercising regularly, become much easier to add to your life.

Shifting your energy source from adrenaline to a healthier fuel takes time. Since our culture promotes a frenetic, frenzied lifestyle, it will take patience and practice to slow your body down. You can begin the process with a few simple (but not necessarily easy) exercises. Try one of the following actions and notice how your body shifts to a slower pace.

### Take Action! Arrive Early

Start arriving fifteen minutes early for every appointment you make. This one action can have a dramatic impact on the adrenaline cycle. Here's how to do it. Take out your appointment book and "ink in" time around any appointment you've made so that you're able to arrive early and relax beforehand. Give yourself room to breathe. Stop trying to cram several things into a small space of time. This so-called efficient use of time causes undo stress and anxiety, raises your adrenaline, and makes you less productive in the long run.

When you schedule new appointments, always add space before and after the allotted time. For example, if you book an appointment from 2 to 3, block out from 1:30 until 3:30. Make this a regular practice, and soon you'll notice that you have more energy—energy that comes from a peaceful, more centered place.

### Take Action! Develop a Daily "Relaxation" Practice

When you decide to kick the adrenaline habit, your body will actually have to learn how to slow down. Like an engine that's been idling too fast for too long, it's as if your body will need to have its timing adjusted. To facilitate this process, try using the following techniques to help slow you down.

LISTEN TO GUIDED RELAXATION TAPES. Listening to a calm voice guiding you into a relaxed state teaches you how to put yourself in that state on demand. As you listen to a tape over and over, you'll train your mind to relax your body when it hears certain words or phrases. After a while, you'll be able to quietly repeat these words or phrases to yourself and use them to relax in any situation. My client Brent found that by listening to one side of a tape twice per day, he was able to put himself into a relaxed state naturally within two weeks. Many clients who were unable to meditate or relax prior to using the tapes were surprised at how easy it was and looked forward to using them each day. In the resource section at the end of this chapter I've listed the two audiotapes that I usually recommend to clients.

TAKE A LONG BATH. Treating your body to a hot bath is another great way to relax. Create a nurturing ritual by adding essential oils like lavender or sandalwood for a calming effect. Be sure that the temperature is just right so you can comfortably sit for a while. Light candles and listen to relaxing music. Create a "spa experience" in the comfort of your own home. If you don't have a suitable bathtub, visit your local health club and sit in the Jacuzzi, sauna, or steam room. My client Heidi, who works out of her home, goes to the gym in the middle of the afternoon when it's slow to meditate in the sauna. Getting used to a relaxed pace will take some time, but give yourself the gift of extreme self-care and make it a priority.

### Take Action! Eliminate Distractions, Interruptions, and Annoyances

Distractions and interruptions—the little things that can be big annoyances—raise your anxiety level and kick in the adrenaline response. Eliminate things that distract you even in subtle ways. For example, schedule time to close your office door to finish work that needs your total concentration. Constant interruptions raise your stress level and keep your body braced for more. Use a "Do Not Disturb" sign on your door that states a time when you'll be available. Let your staff and colleagues know beforehand that you'll be using this method to get things done. This simple strategy did wonders for my client Dorothy, an editor for a national business magazine.

Dorothy complained of never having a chance to get her own writing done because of the constant interruptions from her editorial staff. I suggested that she set a good example for the other writers by creating a "sacred writing" schedule. I asked her to set aside three mornings of uninterrupted time per week to write, and I suggested that she invite her staff to do the same. It took some getting used to—the temptation to want "just a minute" of her time made it necessary for Dorothy to set strict boundaries. But at the end of one month, several members of her staff, along with herself, were meeting their deadlines with ease.

Turn the ringer off on your phone. The telephone that rings while you're working, reading a good book, watching a movie, or trying to sleep will keep your body on edge. Have you ever been startled out of a sound sleep by a ringing phone? The rapid beating of your heart is an indication that the fight-or-flight response has just kicked in. I'm surprised that many people still allow their phones to ring and feel obligated to answer it while they're involved with things that need quiet and concentration. Who said you had to answer your phone just because it rings? Free yourself from this distraction. Give yourself the gift of silence—it can be a great new source of energy.

What distracts or annoys you? Pay attention to the sights and sounds that overstimulate your energy, like a leaky faucet, busy walls, or even a bookcase by your bed. These subtle things pull your attention away and disturb your concentration or relaxation. Spend one week on a search mission looking for these types of things and put them on a list. At the end of the week, review the list and start eliminating them once and for all.

When my client Nathan searched for distractions, he identified several things that annoyed him. The ringer on his phone and the alarm on his clock radio had piercing, shrill sounds. His son's blaring TV in the next room made it difficult to concentrate while Nathan tried to read, and this frustration usually caused a fight. Nathan also felt annoyed by the endless telemarketing phone calls he got and the junk mail stuffed in his mailbox every day.

To handle these distractions, Nathan recruited support from his family. He had his fifteen-year-old daughter make the necessary phone calls to remove them from the junk mail and catalog lists. When the telemarketers called, Nathan instructed his family to tell them to have their number removed from their lists. He also purchased a new phone and alarm clock that had more pleasant tones. Finally, Nathan was thrilled to find a set of cordless headphones that allowed his son to watch TV while Nathan read nearby. Removing these seemingly minor distractions had a significant impact on the quality of Nathan's life.

What's causing you undo stress and raising your adrenaline levels? Eliminate the distractions and consciously set the mood. Like noisy distractions, visual stimulation can raise your anxiety level as well. Just notice what happens when you walk into a busy shopping mall. The lights, the crowds, and the visual images can cause sensory overload. This same kind of overload can happen when your home or office "looks" busy.

You can eliminate this overstimulation by creating what I call "visual clarity." In chapter 3 we discussed ways to eliminate things that drain your energy. Once the clutter is cleared, you can go to the next level by reducing the visual distractions in your home and office. Have you ever walked into a room that had very little furniture or artwork and noticed how calm you felt? Visual clarity not only reduces your stress level but can help to create a soothing environ-

ment that increases the flow of creativity that comes from a relaxed
state of mind.

Survey your environment. As you walk through your home or
office, or even when you get in your car, look at the walls, the desk,
and the floor. Stop and notice how you feel when you look around.
Do you feel relaxed and peaceful, or agitated and overwhelmed?
Now take an inventory and write down the specific changes you'd
like to make:

*Bedroom*

_____
_____

*Office*

_____
_____

*Kitchen*

_____
_____

*Living Area*

_____
_____

*Car*

_____
_____

*Other Areas*

_____
_____

To make changes, experiment with what works for you. See what
it feels like to clear your desktop completely and work on one thing
at a time. File things in a place where you can easily find them. If
you're concerned about losing track of something that needs to get
done, include such items on a "to do" list and review it daily.

Sometimes even favorite mementos can be distracting. As my client Jennifer surveyed her office, she felt overwhelmed by a collage of photos gathered on a bulletin board over her desk. Originally she had hung up a few pictures of herself with friends on a skiing trip to make her smile during the day. But over time, as she added more pictures to the collage, it had gotten much bigger and had now become a visual distraction.

Jennifer decided to put the photos in a scrapbook on a coffee table instead. She also filed away all the paperwork on her desk and hung up a few choice pieces of art that reflected peaceful nature scenes. By creating visual clarity and eliminating distractions, she felt less tired and became far more productive at work.

Lenore created visual clarity in a different way. She noticed her adrenaline kick in whenever she checked her e-mail. Each time she signed on, she had at least twenty messages to read. Lenore admitted that the bulk of her e-mail came from daily and weekly broadcasts. Not only did the amount of mail overwhelm her, but she felt compelled to read everything. She said she felt "bombarded, almost attacked" by new information every day. Although she originally subscribed to these lists to stimulate her thinking, it was now distracting her from her work. Lenore decided to remove herself from 90 percent of the lists and in doing so removed her anxiety too.

### Take Action! Focus Your Energy

Another common way to keep the adrenaline flowing is to spread yourself too thin. Investing your time and energy in too many areas causes stress and anxiety. Instead of working on too many projects at once, pursuing multiple business ideas, or getting involved with too many organizations, narrow your focus. Decide to do one or two things well, and channel your energy. Too many irons in the fire give the illusion of getting a lot accomplished, but it's usually less productive.

One way to focus your energy is to structure your time differently. Plan a specific day or afternoon each week when you'll handle paperwork without interruptions. Then schedule a separate time to return and receive telephone calls. Blocking out chunks of time when you're not required to juggle several different tasks at once not only reduces adrenaline but gets the work done faster.

My client Peggy, a conference planner, completely transformed the way she did business by redesigning her schedule in this way. When Peggy arrived at her office each day, she felt bombarded by the requests for her time. All day long she'd shift focus from the important phone call that needed her immediate attention to the budget that had to be updated and to the program ideas that needed to be generated for her clients. Peggy said that by 3 P.M. she felt wiped and ready for a nap.

I suggested that Peggy set aside three mornings a week to close her door and have her assistant hold all calls. During this time, she worked on the projects that needed her undivided attention, like budget development and proposals. In the afternoon, she got on the phones, answering and returning her calls. Peggy let her clients know that she would be using this new "focus time" to increase her productivity and responsiveness to their needs and asked for their support.

Although at times Peggy felt tempted to take on her clients' crises as her own, she held firm to this new schedule. As a result, she noticed several things: she ate less junk food throughout the day, she felt more present during her conversations with others, and several staff members commented on how much more relaxed the office felt. Routine and structure equal focused energy—a powerful tool for success! Don't confuse busyness with getting closer to your goal—they're two very different things.

As you stop using adrenaline as an energy source, be prepared for some discomfort. Many clients report feeling antsy or bored. This makes sense. Your body is so used to running at high gear that it will feel awkward to slow down. When you start feeling uncomfortable, take this as a sign that you're on the right track. When you're too busy, adrenaline keeps you disconnected from your feelings, the very thing that makes life rich. Don't let life pass you by—it's worth the temporary discomfort.

A final note about adrenaline—if you find it too difficult to slow down, make an appointment with a good holistic physician and have your adrenal system tested. You may be a good candidate for the various supplements available to support adrenal health.

Don't get pulled back into the adrenaline trap. Get support from your coaching partner or group. Commit to the actions that will help you kick the adrenaline habit, and report back on your progress during your next meeting. This will help you to stay on track. Since the push to induce a high adrenaline state is never ending in our culture, it takes vigilance with new habits put firmly in place to stop running on adrenaline.

———

Now let's look at energy that comes from a higher source—the kinds of fuel that give you the power to do all that you want to do and contribute to your overall health and well-being. Living a high-quality, whole life is a long-distance event. Give yourself plenty of the good fuel you need to sustain yourself. Review the What's Fueling You? list below and check the good fuel sources already in your life.

### What's Fueling You?

*Relationships*

_____ I enjoy the company of special friends.

_____ I share my life with a soulmate.

_____ I have a blood family or chosen family with whom I feel close.

_____ I get immense pleasure from spending time with children.

_____ I have a pet that brings me joy and provides me with unconditional love.

_____ I spend time having fun with people who make me laugh.

_____ I am part of a loving and supportive community.

_____ I have relationships that stimulate me intellectually.

_____ I have people I can turn to in times of need.

_____ I have relationships where I feel intimately connected to others.

## Environment

_____ I have a special "soul nurturing" place in my home just for me.

_____ I listen to my favorite music regularly.

_____ I love my sense of style and feel good in the clothes I wear.

_____ I've let go of all the "stuff" I no longer need.

_____ I keep fresh flowers in my home and office.

_____ My home is neat, clean, and well organized.

_____ I create beauty around me.

_____ I love the neighborhood I live in.

_____ My bedroom is the perfect place to get a good night's sleep.

_____ I have at least one room with a beautiful view that I enjoy.

## Body, Mind, and Spirit

_____ I exercise regularly.

_____ I have eliminated caffeine from my diet.

_____ I have a way to relax that eliminates stress and keeps me feeling centered.

_____ I eat healthy and nutritious foods.

_____ I care for my body with regular healthcare checkups and bodywork appointments.

_____ Each day I read something inspirational to keep my attitude positive.

_____ I have a spiritual practice that connects me with my Wise Self.

_____ I feel a strong connection to a power greater than myself.

_____ I set aside regular time for solitude and silence.

_____ I have a safe and healthy outlet for my emotional well-being.

*Work*

_____ I enjoy my work.

_____ My commute is stress free.

_____ I have a mentor who guides and encourages me.

_____ I always take lunch breaks.

_____ I have colleagues who inspire and respect me.

_____ I take mental health days when I need them.

_____ I feel energized at the end of most work days.

_____ My office is a beautiful space that's well organized and free from distractions.

_____ My work contributes to a larger vision that I have for my life.

_____ My ideas and talents are welcome at work.

*Money*

_____ I always carry enough cash with me.

_____ I have a system to keep my finances in order, and I know where my money goes.

_____ I am fully insured and protected.

_____ I save money consistently.

_____ My taxes are paid and up to date.

_____ I've made smart investments that earn me top dollar.

_____ I enjoy being generous and easily share my wealth.

_____ I pay myself first.

_____ I spend my money on things that I love.

_____ I pay my credit cards in full each month.

These are the things that will fuel you in a way that contributes to the quality of your life. Using the same scoring process in chapter 3, give yourself 2 points for every item checked. Tally each section individually and multiply by 2. Then, combine the scores from each section for a grand total. With 100 points available, how did you do? If your score is low, don't worry. Now that you have more time and energy available, it will be easier to consistently add more of these types of energy sources to your life.

My client Ken was surprised at how easy it was to change his work habits once he stopped running on adrenaline. Ken was a division manager for a Fortune 100 company. He decided to change his weekly routine by intentionally adding healthy sources of energy while at his job. Ken chose to add more physical activity to his week and develop a stronger sense of community with his coworkers. He made a commitment to himself to no longer work through lunch, eating candy bars and drinking coffee. Instead, he started running three times a week, and on the days when he wasn't running he invited his coworkers to join him for lunch at a nearby salad bar.

During their lunches, Ken got to know his colleagues better. Rather than spend time on "shop talk," he made a point to inquire about their personal lives. He discovered that he and his colleagues had many things in common. One coworker was dealing with the challenge of placing an aging parent in a nursing home, and Ken, having gone through the same thing two years earlier, offered his advice and support. Another loved baseball, Ken's favorite sport, and they instantly began comparing notes about their favorite players. He said he looked forward to these lunches and, as a result, found himself energized during the second half of the day and really enjoying his job.

## PREMIUM FUEL

Let's look at how you can add new premium fuel to your life. There are three areas that I'd like you to focus on:

*Fuel your body.*
*Fuel your mind.*
*Fuel your spirit.*

## Take Action! Fuel Your Body

Caring for your body is essential to living a high-quality life. Fuel your body with premium fuel and it will provide you with the strength and stamina to live well. As you start to get your life in shape, you'll find that your body often follows. Many clients who get their priorities straight and start to heal their lives lose unwanted weight and naturally heal their bodies.

With thousands of books available on health and fitness, I don't need to tell you how to care for your body. As a matter of fact, I rarely offer advice on those types of issues—I leave it for the professionals. I do, however, recommend specific strategies to help clients fuel their bodies in fun and nurturing ways. I encourage you to try some of the following exercises.

**MAKE HEALTHY EATING EASY.** Food is a direct fuel source for the body. Like gasoline for our cars, good food keeps the body running well. But eating healthy can be a challenge. If you struggle with a weight problem or eating well, find a partner to support you. Millions of people battle with weight and eating well. The billions of dollars spent each year on diet books and exercise equipment make it obvious that the "one size fits all" mentality doesn't work. For most, food is a very personal and loaded issue.

Find a nutritionist, a partner, who will help you to learn what types of food serve your body best. This person should assist you in creating a personal way of eating that supports who you are. Build on what you already do well. Let his or her ongoing support help you to put new patterns in place. Be sure that your nutritionist is not only well trained in nutrition but also skilled with the emotional and life issues that are often connected with food.

Most of us, if we listen to our Wise Selves, already know some of the foods that are better for us than others. What good food do you already include in your diet that you could add more of? Which food would you like to eat less of?

*Foods I'd like to eat less of:*  *Foods I'd like to eat more of:*

_____  _____

_____  _____

_____  _____

_____  _____

Pick one food you know you should eat less of and replace it with a better food over the next thirty days. Make gradual changes. If you drink too much coffee, cut back by mixing caffeinated and decaffeinated together. Or, if a donut is your daily snack on the way to work, replace it with a better choice, like a whole-grain bagel. What simple changes can you start to make now?

Look for ways to make eating healthy easier. Several "green" drinks, like barley green and spirulina, provide instant nutrition and also reduce sugar and carbohydrate cravings (see the resource section for suggestions). This type of high-powered nutrition can be great when you're busy and tempted to snack on junk food.

Hire a personal cook. When my husband and I added up all the money spent on eating out and grabbing a quick lunch here and there, we discovered that hiring a cook to prepare and deliver healthy, nutritious meals to our home was actually less expensive (under $150 for the week—including food!). We designed a simple flyer and posted it at our local health food store and found the perfect person within one week. At times when we're too busy to cook a healthy meal, we simply open the refrigerator and warm up something already prepared.

Try new healthy foods. It's much easier to replace an unhealthy food with a better choice when you have new foods that you love to choose from. Experiment with new foods by taking cooking classes, collecting recipes from friends, or buying a great cookbook. My client Ginger discovered that she loved Vietnamese food, a cuisine low in fat and filled with lots of fresh vegetables and flavorful spices.

A local restaurant owner agreed to tutor her in the art of Vietnamese cooking, and along with a good cookbook, she made healthy eating fun and creative!

**MAKE EXERCISE FUN.** I know you know this, so consider it a friendly reminder: get your body moving! Good exercise fuels your body, mind, and spirit. Exercise can become a tool for reconnecting with your body in ways that are both nurturing and fun. Why not try something new and different? For example, try some of the new cardiovascular options that are now available at most gyms. Go for a ride on the "spinning" bikes or climb the rock wall. So what if you're fifty and haven't been on a bike since you were fifteen—take a risk, give it a try!

Use the great outdoor gym that is always available. Take a hike up a mountain or at least climb some hills. Find a park and try mountain biking (you can rent a bike at first), or join a runners club and run with a "built in" team. If you work in the city, go out and take in the sights. I find that clients are able to stick with exercise when they do three things: do something they really enjoy, do it with a friend, and add variety along the way.

Making exercise fun and interesting will help keep you motivated. To do this, you might try connecting with a fun form of recreation from your past. Pierce, a client who worked out regularly, often talked about the "good old days" of baseball during his high school years. One day during a coaching session, I asked him if there were any baseball leagues in his area. He admitted that he occasionally thought about joining a local team but was sure it was too late. He suggested, "I haven't played in so long that I probably wouldn't be able to hit the ball very far, let alone throw it."

I asked Pierce to humor me and make a few calls just for the heck of it to check it out. When he located an over-thirty men's league with openings, I then asked him to go to one practice and give it a shot. That's all it took. After one attempt, he was hooked. It's been two years now, and Pierce is one of the top hitters on his team.

Is there a sport or activity that you could resurrect? Something that you love to do? One of my clients combined her love of gospel with exercise when she found a "gospel" aerobics class on the other side of town. Now, not only does she raise her heart rate but she lifts her spirits as well. Try something new, like these:

| | |
|---|---|
| *Water aerobics* | *Volleyball* |
| *Rollerblading* | *Ice skating* |
| *Swimming* | *Squash/racquetball* |
| *Hiking* | *Cross-country skiing* |

My client Connie had a hard time sticking with any exercise until she was introduced to country/western dancing by a friend. She was a bit reluctant at first but decided to take a few lessons and give it a try. Connie was a natural! She loved the music, learned the steps easily, and started dancing three nights a week. She said it was the most fun exercising she'd had in a long time.

If you're the type of person who gets bored easily, make sure you add variety to your exercise routine. Take a brisk walk on one day, visit the gym on the next, and try hiking on the weekends. Stop thinking of exercise as an option. Start thinking of it as a daily part of your routine of self-care. The benefits of exercise—like maintaining a healthy weight that contributes to longevity, building stronger bones, and creating more energy—are easy to forget because they're cumulative rather than immediate. Start to think of daily exercise as a deposit to your long-term health and well-being. After all, when you stop beating yourself up for not exercising, the peace of mind is well worth the daily deposit.

**PAMPER YOUR BODY.** In the spirit of extreme self-care, pamper and care for your body on a regular basis. Schedule a massage or some other form of bodywork to help your body relax and rejuvenate. In the past, getting a massage was considered either a luxury or a necessary treatment for injury. Today, with our increased levels of stress and our sedentary (but frantic!) lifestyles, our bodies hold far more tension and anxiety. This has made massage and other forms of bodywork (like reiki and reflexology) important ways to fuel our bodies.

Bodywork restores balance, gets the circulation flowing, and increases your energy. There are several types of bodywork you can try, from regular massage to hot oil treatments and herbal wraps. Experiment and find the ones that suit you best. You might want to try some of these:

*Massage: Swedish, shiatsu, therapeutic touch*
*Chiropractic care*
*Cranial sacral work*
*Energy work: polarity, reiki, acupuncture*
*Facial, manicure, pedicure*
*Herbal wraps and scrubs*
*Reflexology*

If you've never had a bodywork treatment, don't let unknown fears stop you from indulging in this wonderful form of self-care. Often, clients have privately shared their concerns about needing to remove their clothes during bodywork. But extreme self-care means you're always in charge. Decide what you need to feel safe. Let the massage therapist or practitioner know that you'd like to remain fully clothed, or start out by trying one of the treatments that are done fully clothed, like polarity or foot reflexology.

In the beginning, treat yourself to some form of bodywork at least once a month. Schedule several months in advance so you always have an appointment waiting for you. Eventually, as you experience the powerful impact this can have on your health, you'll want to increase the frequency. You deserve to have your body well taken care of. Bodywork is no longer a luxury, it's a standard. Book a treatment today!

GET A GOOD NIGHT'S SLEEP. A good night's sleep is just as critical a fuel as food, water, and exercise. More than 30 percent of my clients have had trouble with getting consistent good sleep, and I have witnessed the resulting depressions, immune-related illnesses, low energy, and fatigue. Sleep is a key fuel source for the body that often gets overlooked or underemphasized until there's a problem. Without regular, sound rest, it's impossible to enjoy life fully.

Do you wake feeling refreshed and well rested? Is your bedroom an optimal place for rest and relaxation? What do you need to get a good night's sleep? Aside from a high-quality mattress and the right pillows, which we all know are the basics for good sleep, there are other things to consider.

What's the air quality like in your bedroom? Poor air quality (especially in the winter months, when the heat is on) can make sleeping difficult. If you wake sneezing, coughing, feeling foggy, or with sinus headaches, a stuffy nose, or dry, red, or puffy eyes, you may be experiencing symptoms of poor air quality that will prevent you from sleeping soundly. Try using an air filter to purify the air in your bedroom. Also, move anything that's plugged into an electric current at least three feet away from your bed to reduce the electrical field of electromagnetic radiation. This can contribute to headaches and fogginess as well.

Eliminate unwanted noise by using a "white noise" machine or an audiotape with sounds like ocean waves or gentle rain. Let your bedroom become a sanctuary. Be sure it's clean, dust free, and decorated in a way that makes you feel calm and peaceful. Go to bed when you feel tired. Forget about watching TV or doing work in bed. Let this be a quiet time to fuel your body with rest.

If you have a hard time falling asleep, do something to relax beforehand—take a hot bath, listen to music with your eyes closed, talk to someone you love, or read. Turn off your head. If you find it difficult to sleep because of the noise in your head, use your relaxation tapes to help lull you to sleep. If you need to, seek the help of a sleep specialist. The investment of time and money is well worth it. Fuel your body with good sleep—your health and your life depend on it.

TAKE A DEEP BREATH. Finally, don't forget your body's most important fuel of all—your breath. Most of us, especially when we lead busy lives, get in the habit of breathing only into the upper chest area. But your body needs deep breathing to oxygenate the blood and increase energy. The simple act of breathing down into your belly can instantly make you feel more relaxed and alive at the same time.

Try it—stop right now and take a deep breath down into your belly so that your stomach moves outward. Do this three or four times. Breathe in through your nose, count to four on the in breath, hold for a count of eight, and then breath out through your nose slowly to a count of two. Notice how you feel. Deep breathing is a great exercise to do while waiting at a red light, sitting at your desk, or just before going to sleep.

### Take Action! Fuel Your Mind

Like your body, your mind needs to be fed as well. Reading great books, participating in stimulating conversation, and learning something new are all great ways to fuel your mind, but the most powerful fuel of all is the thoughts that you think.

For decades, hundreds of books have been written about the power of thought to create physical reality. Thought becomes intention, this intention has power, and when you put this intention out into the world, your life starts to change—sometimes dramatically. This is a basic metaphysical law.

When I first talk to clients about the power of thought, I share a personal experience that taught me to take this age-old truth seriously. As a young woman, I loved reading books by some of the great early success writers. I was captivated and inspired by the simple wisdom of Emmett Fox, Robert Collier, Napolean Hill, Florence Scovel Shinn, and Norman Vincent Peale. Each author shared a deep, spiritual conviction that our lives could be transformed by the quality of our thoughts. I was especially interested in the practical tools they offered as a way to bring about this personal transformation.

MAKE A WISH LIST. One of the first tools I tried was to put a few simple goals in writing and refer to them regularly to keep the thoughts alive in my mind. Always the skeptic, I wanted to see if this really worked, so I started with a simple wish list, which included a computer with the exact specifications and software that I preferred (I read that it was important to be as specific as possible when setting goals), free travel, and the elimination of my debt. I made this list in October and put it in the front of my appointment book, knowing that I would see it several times each day.

Two months later, I received a Christmas gift from a client. Instead of a monetary bonus, he said he wanted to give me something "a writer could really use." When I opened the box, my chin fell as I sat speechless looking at the exact computer I had put on my list. One month later, a friend called to tell me about a contest she had won at work. The prize was an all-expense-paid trip for two to one of the finest hotels in the United States, and she wondered if I might like to go along. Again I was shocked. Committing my thoughts to paper and holding the intention by reviewing them every day created a state of attraction that drew these goals into my life. Coincidence or not, this was all the proof I needed to start taking more seriously the power of intentionally fueling my mind with certain thoughts. Needless to say, I began a new list.

Try it for yourself. Stop a moment and think about three things you would most like to attract. Now write them here:

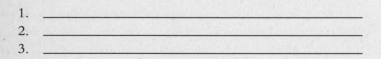

1. _____
2. _____
3. _____

Be specific. If you want to make more money, write down the exact amount and include a "+" sign after it (you never know, you may get more). If you'd like a new apartment, describe your ideal place.

Now write these three items on a 3"-×-5" index card and keep them with you. Glance at your wish list throughout the day and imagine yourself already having these things. Don't be too attached to the results, just be mindful of them. If you have any concerns about limiting yourself by being too specific or if you're afraid that there may be something better for you that you haven't yet thought of, simply say a little prayer asking that "this or better come into my life."

Pay attention to what happens. My clients are often amazed by the results. One client, Robert, made a list that included a better-paying job and a great relationship. Eight months later, while vacationing with friends in the Caribbean, he met a woman who, coincidentally, lived two hours from his home in a nearby state. Over the next year, they fell in love, they bought a home in her neighborhood, and he started a new job with a higher salary.

CREATE A TREASURE MAP. A treasure map is another great way to keep your mind fueled with what really matters. In 1948, Robert Collier, in his book *The Secret of the Ages,* introduced the concept of creating a "treasure map" as a way to visualize those things that you'd like to have in your life. A treasure map is a collage of visual images that can reflect the items on your Absolute Yes list. For example, if your physical health is a priority, you may want to include images of exercise equipment, the outdoors, Rollerblades, or a bicycle. If fun and adventure are a priority, you might have pictures of a place you'd like to visit or an adventure like white-water rafting or mountain climbing. You can also include your material goals (a new car or appliance) and your relationship goals.

This treasure map, kept in a place where you can see it daily, will send a clear message to your subconscious and the Universe of your intentions. The magnetic power of holding these intentions in mind, Collier suggests, will attract what you most desire into your life.

Make sure your images include goals for your whole life: health, work, relationships, fun, and financial goals. Creating a treasure map is a great project for you and your coaching partner or group. Hold a treasure map party and have each member bring the following supplies: a large piece of foam core board, scissors, several catalogs and magazines, glue, and magic markers. Start by cutting out pictures from catalogs and magazines of things that you'd like to attract into your life. Then, glue these images onto your board in a way that is visually appealing to you. And finally, add any affirmations, words, or special sayings that inspire you.

When creating your treasure map, remember to always use the "+" sign or the words "or more" for any dollar amounts that reflect your earnings and savings goals. For example, if you'd like to earn $50,000 in income, put the following on your treasure map: $50,000+. You never know what might be in store for you. My client Russell was amazed to find a bonus check from his employer in his mailbox in the middle of the summer. The company had had a particularly good fiscal year and decided to surprise their employees by sharing the wealth. Russell had placed a savings goal of $1,000+ for the year on his treasure map and was pleasantly surprised when he received a check for $1,500.

Use words creatively. Put the word "free" in front of other words or pictures. For example, if you use the word "travel" or "rent," add "free" to it—"free travel" or "free rent." When my client Sandy created her treasure map with a group of friends, she included a "free apartment" because she knew that she needed to move at the end of the year. Two months after completing her map, Sandy was offered an in-law apartment by a family friend in exchange for the occasional care of an elderly woman. This meant she would live rent free! Make your treasure map personal, inspiring, and a joy to look at. And be sure to take note of the things that show up in your life.

**THINK HIGH-QUALITY THOUGHTS.** If thought has the power to create reality, then to create a high-quality life you'll want to fuel your mind with high-quality thoughts. Learning to raise your thinking to a higher level is a lifelong process that takes patience and practice. By using a few specific tools, you can start to influence your thinking in a gradual and positive way.

Pay attention to what you say to yourself. All clients I have ever worked with have a tendency to be hard on themselves. Negative self-talk is debilitating and has absolutely no value. If you find yourself thinking things like, "I'm not good enough," or "I can't have what I really want," or "I never do anything right," replace these thoughts immediately with a preplanned affirmation or mantra. For example, the statement "I deeply and profoundly accept myself" is a powerful message to give yourself. Most negative self-talk revolves around an inability to fully accept our normal human imperfections. This one statement of self-acceptance may actually shift the body's energy field into a state of balance that improves immune functioning.

Create your own self-loving mantra. What one statement would you say to someone you deeply loved and cared about who was giving himself or herself a hard time? Write that phrase below:

---

Now every time you catch yourself using negative self-talk, immediately replace the thought with this new mantra. Not only will it remind you to go easy on yourself, but it may actually improve your physical health as well.

Choose inspirational reading that keeps your mind focused on positive, healthy thoughts. Many daily affirmation books are filled with inspiring material to lift your thoughts and raise your spirits. Find a book that you love and keep one at work, in your car, or by your bed, and read a page throughout the day. Subscribe to an inspirational e-mail list to receive messages daily or weekly (see the resource section at the end of this chapter for addresses).

Display visual messages around you by keeping simple words, phrases, or images hung on a wall or bulletin board in your home or office. Words like "faith," "joy," and "love" can have a powerful, subliminal effect on your mind. Pick one or two simple words or phrases, write them in big letters on a blank piece of paper, and keep them near you. Once again, keep it simple. Don't put too many around. Focus on one word a week, and then change the word. Or use a catchy phrase to reinforce a desired belief. For example, some of the phrases I often recommend to clients are: "Be yourself, don't play it safe," "Abundance is my birthright" and "What I desire is possible." Fill your mind with good thoughts, and you'll reap the rewards.

Turn off the junk. Pay close attention to what gets in your mind. Make a conscious choice about the newspapers and magazines that you read. There is a growing body of research that suggests that negative images actually suppress the body's immune system. I'm sure you've felt it—the strong gut reaction to a visual image of violence or a story of crime or tragedy. If you feel it in your body, you know it's affecting your emotional and physical health. As you become more connected to your feelings, you'll need to protect yourself from these types of negative fuel. Stop feeding your mind the nightly news before going to bed. Fuel your mind with premium fuel. Remember, after the thought, there is intention, and from intention springs power, the power to create your whole, healthy, happy life.

## Take Action! Fuel Your Spirit

Fuel your spirit, and life takes on a magical quality that can fill each moment with joy. Although I've devoted an entire chapter to honoring your spiritual well-being, here I'd like to offer you specific ways to reawaken and rejuvenate the part of you that often gets lost in a busy life—your spirit.

**LISTEN TO YOUR FAVORITE MUSIC.** Rediscover the music of your younger years. Stop and think about your adolescent years, the years when you were in high school, college, and beyond. What music did you love? What were your favorite songs and performers? I'm sure you've had the experience of listening to the radio and being suddenly sent back in time by hearing an old favorite song. Music can be an instant state changer that fuels your spirit and makes you feel great. I'd like you to reach back into your past and bring back the positive, uplifting songs that you loved. Stop and remember five of your favorite songs or performers and write them here:

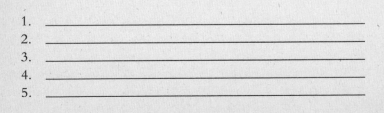

1. _____
2. _____
3. _____
4. _____
5. _____

Listening to old favorites can instantly inspire you and bring back fond memories. Music can be a powerful, emotional force that makes you feel empowered and strong, happy and full of life. Make a date to go to your local music shop and find these songs. My client Jonathan gathered his favorite songs and made a cassette tape that he keeps in his car. Whenever he feels down, frustrated, or upset in any way, he takes out the tape and has an instant change of heart. My client Rose loved Christmas music and found that it put her in a celebratory mood. Instead of waiting until the holidays, Rose decided that it was perfectly fine to listen to Christmas carols in the summertime.

**LIFT YOUR SPIRITS WITH LAUGHTER.** Get together with friends who make you laugh; read a funny book; or see a comedy show. Give yourself the luxury of a good belly laugh every once in a while. Not only is laughter fun but it's a powerful healing agent as well. Stop taking life so seriously. Laugh a little! If you want help getting started, rent a funny video. Think of it as "laugh therapy." Give yourself a dose at least once a week. When I asked my clients to recommend their favorite movies and TV shows, they suggested these:

**TV:**
*Seinfeld, Fraiser, Friends, I Love Lucy, All in the Family, Gilligan's Island, Mash, Carol Burnett*
*Johnny Carson* tapes
*Saturday Night Live* videos (from the early 1980s)
**Movies:**
*Liar, Liar*
*The Gallagher Comedy Series*
*Birdcage*
*The Full Monty*
*Caddy Shack*

**HAVE A GOOD CRY.** This may seem like a strange way to fuel your spirit, but a good cry can make a world of difference.

Freeing pent-up emotions in the body can help to clear energy blocks that prevent your spirit from fully experiencing joy. When my client Allison feels irritable, she knows it's a sign that she's in need of a good cry. She curls up in bed when no one is home and cries. She says it cleanses her soul.

There's a saying that a good belly laugh lives on the other side of a good cry. Crying helps to clean out the mind, reenergize the body, and rejuvenate the spirit. Many people find it difficult to cry. If you'd like a gentle nudge, rent a sad movie and watch it in the privacy of your home (when you're alone) and let yourself go. I often recommend a list of sad movies for those clients who say they feel like they need a good cry. These movies include the following:

> *My Life*
> *Terms of Endearment*
> *Love Story*
> *When a Man Loves a Woman*
> *Dying Young*
> *Table for Five*
> *Beaches*
> *Steel Magnolias*
> *Bridges of Madison County*

If crying seems impossible, look for other safe ways to let out your pent-up emotions and free your spirit. Josh, a client who said it was impossible for him to cry, found that visiting a batting cage was an effective way to express his emotions and fuel his spirit. Whenever he felt overwhelmed, he went to the batting cages and hit baseballs until his arms were tired. When he finished, Josh said he felt a total release that made him feel lighter.

**BE OUTRAGEOUS.** Fuel your spirit by doing something wild and extravagant. Send yourself a bunch of gorgeous flowers and spread them around your home or office. Treat yourself like you would the most attractive, thoughtful, sexy, funny, and caring person you could meet. Buy yourself a set of silk sheets. Go to a restaurant for dinner, pretend it's your birthday, and let them bring out a cake and sing to you! Buy a bunch of coloring books and crayons and invite friends over for a coloring contest. See how well you color *outside* the lines.

Try something you haven't done before. Take a dance class and learn the tango, or buy a small journal and write a book. Take a risk and paint a room a bold color, like red or purple. Get a completely different haircut or color, and see what it's like to look different. Your spirit needs this kind of fuel. Most of all, break out of the pattern of "appropriate" behavior, and live out loud!

**DO SOMETHING YOU'VE ALWAYS WANTED TO DO.** We all secretly harbor things that we'd love to do, have been meaning to do, or are afraid to do. Sometimes a busy life gets in the way. Other times, it just seems easier to keep putting these secret desires on the back burner. Search your heart and look for those things that you've always wanted to do. To help you discover your unfulfilled desires, take out your journal and answer the questions below. Let your imagination run wild—don't hold yourself back with practical concerns.

*Is there a place you've always wanted to visit? If so, where?*

_____

*Are there people that you'd love to spend more time with? If so, whom?*

_____

*Is there a hobby that you've wanted to begin or spend more time on? If so, what?*

_____

*If you had one free day to spend spontaneously doing whatever you desire, what would you do?*

_____

*Are there books you'd love to read? If so, which ones?*

_____

*Is there a new sport or physical activity you'd like to try (even
    if it scares you a little)? If so, what?*

_____

*Is there a class or workshop you've been meaning to take? If
    so, which one?*

_____

*Would you love to learn about a different culture? If so, which
    one? How will you do it?*

_____

*Is there a new career direction you'd like to explore? If so,
    what? How will you begin?*

_____

*What else have you always wanted to do?*

_____

The next important question is: When will you do these things?
What are you waiting for? Pick one and take action within the next
twenty-four hours. It can be a small action—a first step toward fulfilling that desire—but any action will take you closer to doing these
things and will give you an immediate boost. Fuel your spirit and let
it soar!

## REPLACE THE OLD WITH THE NEW

Now that you've learned some healthy ways to fuel your body, mind,
and spirit, start to replace any old energy sources that no longer serve
you with new healthy ones that will. Many sources of energy will

fuel you *and* protect your health. Instead of watching the violence and drama of the evening news, pop in a funny video or go to bed early and get some extra rest. Stop working through lunch; get out and walk in the fresh air. You'll find it easier to let go of the junk fuels by adding more of the premium variety.

As you start to feel more in charge of what's fueling you, be kind to yourself. Don't beat yourself up when you slip back into using the old energy sources. New behaviors take time. The goal is the process, and when you get off track just get back on and continue forward. Being hard on yourself will only perpetuate a vicious cycle that's sure to make you fail.

You deserve to fuel yourself with the best. Enjoy life fully by running on premium fuel. In the next chapter I'll show you how to energize your life with one of the best fuel sources of all—soulful relationships.

COACHING REMINDERS
*You deserve to fuel your life with the best—run on premium!*

- Kick the adrenaline habit with these simple steps:
  Arrive early.
  Develop a daily relaxation practice.
  Eliminate distractions, interruptions, and annoyances.
  Focus your energy.
- Run on premium fuel:
  Fuel your body.
  Fuel your mind.
  Fuel your spirit.

# RESOURCES

*BOOKS*

**Succulent Wild Woman: Dancing with Your Wonder-Full Self** by SARK
     (New York: Fireside Books, 1997)
This delightful book, handwritten and painted by the inimitable SARK,
exults in the pleasure of living life to its fullest.

**Women's Bodies, Women's Wisdom** by Christiane Northrup (New York:
     Bantam Books, 1998)
I recommend this book to every woman I work with. From A to Z, this
book contains everything you'd want to know about women's health from a
well-rounded holistic/traditional perspective. A must read for every woman.

**Enter the Zone** by Barry Sears and Bill Lawren (New York: ReganBooks,
     1995)
Developed by respected researcher and health consultant Dr. Barry Sears,
this program is a lifelong, lasting weight-loss plan based on a simple, nonre-
strictive diet with easy-to-follow steps that link food to hormone
"switches" in the body.

**8 Weeks to Optimum Health** by Andrew Weil (New York: Alfred A. Knopf,
     1997)
This book provides an excellent, practical, step-by-step plan for enhancing
and protecting your health.

**When Working Out Isn't Working Out** by Michael Gerrish (New York: St.
     Martin's Press, 1999)
A cutting-edge fitness guide that reveals unidentified fitness obstacles.

**How to Get a Good Night's Sleep: More Than 100 Ways You Can Improve
     Your Sleep** by Richard Garber and Paul Gouin (Minneapolis:
     Chronimed Publishing, 1995)

**Power Through Constructive Thinking** by Emmet Fox (San Francisco:
     HarperSanFrancisco, 1989)
Fox shows how, through constructive thinking, we may achieve the per-

sonal power to overcome failure and discouragement, opening the way to a fuller, richer life.

***The Power of Positive Thinking*** by Norman Vincent Peale (New York: Fawcett Book Group, 1996)
Filled with inspiring stories and spiritual wisdom, this book is a classic.

***Think and Grow Rich*** by Napoleon Hill (New York: Fawcett Book Group, 1996)
The world's number one motivational book tells how to be a winner. Hill has inspired millions to make their dreams come true.

***Secret of the Ages*** by Robert Collier (New York: Robert Collier Publications, 1984)
One of the best books ever written on the power of thought.

## NURTURING ENVIRONMENTS

### The Feng Shui Guild
http://www.fengshuiguild.com
(303) 444-1548
info@fengshuiguild.com
For practitioner referrals and more information on how you can create a nurturing environment using feng shui principles.

***Sacred Space—Creating and Enhancing the Energy of Your Home*** by Denise Linn (New York: Ballantine Books, 1995)
In this book, Denise shows you how you can dramatically change your life by changing the environment in your home or office.

## HEALTH-RELATED RESOURCES

### Dr. Christiane Northrup's "Health Wisdom for Women" Newsletter
Phillips Publishing, Inc.
7811 Montrose Rd.

Potomac, MD 20854
(800) 804–0935
Twelve Issues for $39.95

**Dr. Andrew Weil's "Self Healing" Newsletter**
P.O. Box 792
Mt. Morris, IL 61054–8468
(800) 337–9345
Twelve issues for $29

**SARK's "Magic Museletter"**
Eight issues for $23
Payable by check only, write to:
Camp SARK, Attn: Museletter
P.O. Box 33039
San Francisco, CA 94133

**The Austin HealthMate Air Purifier**
Phillips Publishing, Inc.
7811 Montrose Rd.
P.O. Box 59750
Potomac, MD 20859–9750
(800) 705–5559

**Dr. Glen Rothfeld**
American Whole Health
180 Massachusetts Ave., Suite 303
Arlington, MA 02174
(781) 641–1901
   Rothfeld offers information and telephone consultations on a wide variety of health-related issues including adrenal system tests.

**Hale Baycu-Schatz**
P.O. Box 504
Lexington, MA 02173
(781) 863–9997

Hale is a nutritional educator and consultant who helps individuals find their own unique way of eating for optimal health. Available to work with clients by telephone, she maintains a national practice of individuals and groups.

## MASSAGE AND OTHER RELATED BODYWORK

**American Massage Therapy Association (A.M.T.A.)**
820 Davis St., Suite 100
Evanston, IL 60201–4444
(847) 864–0123
www.amtamassage.org
This organization provides state referral telephone numbers to locate a massage therapist in your area.

**Associated Bodywork and Massage Professionals (A.B.M.P.)**
28677 Buffalo Park Rd.
Evergreen, CO 80439–7347
(800) 458–2267
www.abmp.com
This organization provides local referrals for massage therapists as well as other types of bodyworkers.

**American Polarity Therapy Association (A.P.T.A.)**
2888 Bluff St., #149
Boulder, CO 80301
(303) 545–2080
www.polaritytherapy.org
This organization provides referrals for polarity therapists in your area.

**Healing Hands**
849 Lexington Ave.
New York, NY 10021
(800) 636–7360
This organization dispatches massage therapists to private homes and hotels in Los Angeles, New York, San Francisco, West Palm Beach, and Miami Beach and may be able to provide a therapist in your area.

## RELAXATION TAPES

**Peggy Huddleston**
"Prepare for Surgery, Heal Faster" audiotape
$9.95 plus shipping and handling
http://www.healfaster.com
(800) 726–4173

> Although this tape was originally used for patients undergoing surgery, it has become popular with a wider audience through word of mouth. The tape does not mention anything about surgery, and Peggy's calming voice guides the listener through a twenty-minute relaxation process that has powerful results. Not only will you find it easier to relax, but you'll find it has a positive impact on your overall health.

**Brian Weiss**
"Healing Meditation"
"Meditation to Inner Peace, Love, and Joy"
http://www.brianweiss.com
(305) 661–6610

> Weiss, author of *Many Lives, Many Masters,* and *Only Love Is Real,* is a Yale-trained psychiatrist and pioneer in the field of past life regression therapy. Guided by his hypnotic, soothing voice, each of these tapes will lead you into a state of bliss.

## OTHER RELAXING MUSIC

Enya—"Shepherd Moon"
Yanni—"Reflections of Passion"
Narada—"Decade—The Anniversary Collection"
Liz Story—"Solid Colors"

## HIGH-POWERED NUTRITIONAL GREEN DRINKS

### Barleygreen
AIM International
3904 E. Flamingo Ave.
Nampa, ID 83687–3100
(800) 456–2462

This nutritious drink has been a lifesaver for me when I'm busy and want to be sure that I'm fueling myself with good food. One teaspoon of organically grown Barleygreen is equal to two heads of broccoli.

### PureSynergy Superfood
The Synergy Company
CVSR Box 2901
Moab, UT 84532
(800) 723–0277
http://www.synergy-co.com

This Superfood is a powerful combination of ingredients that include several forms of algae, Chinese and Western herbs, Asian mushrooms, spirulina, and more to provide another easy way to fuel yourself with premium nutrition.

## DANCING

**http://www.io.com/~entropy/contradance/web-page-index.html**
This site provides a geographic listing of contra dance groups.

**http://www.idir.net/usdanew/sdlinks.htm**
This site provides information about square dancing, contra dancing, clogging, and round dance clubs around the world.

## SLEEP

### National Sleep Foundation
http://www.sleepfoundation.org
  The National Sleep Foundation is a nonprofit organization dedicated to enhancing the quality of life for the millions of Americans who suffer from sleep disorders.

## GAMES

### Mindpack—McQuaig Group
### Trivial Pursuit—Parker Brothers
### Jeopardy—Tiger Electronics

## MOVIES

### Blockbuster Video
http://www.blockbuster.com

## TRAVEL RESOURCES

### Specialty Travel Index
http://www.specialtytravel.com
  Provides detailed information about thousands of unusual vacations, offered by over six hundred tour operators and outfitters around the globe.

### Wild Women: A Touring Company
http://www.wildwomenadv.com/wwcom.html
  A unique travel company that arranges hassle-free trips for small groups of women. They are dedicated to the proposition that you can restore, energize, and empower yourself while exploring the world.

### The Green Travel Network
http://www.greentravel.com

**Spa Finders**

http://www.spafinders.com

**Custom Spa Vacations**

http://www.spatours.com

Vacations worldwide for fitness, relaxation, beauty, stress reduction, weight loss, and lifestyle changes. International spas combine spa vacations with interesting sites.

*INSPIRATION*

**Inspire**

http://www.infoadvn.com/inspire

A free daily e-mail broadcast that gives inspirational quotes. Give a gift subscription to a friend!

**Daily Motivator**

http://www.greatday.com

Great motivational messages delivered to you in e-mail six days a week. $15/year.

# 6

---

# Build

# a Soulful

# Community

---

Carla came to our coaching session very upset. The night before, she and her boyfriend had been to see the movie *Soulfood,* and it had touched her deeply. The movie focused on the lives of an African American family struggling to stay connected throughout life's inevitable challenges. While dealing with death, infidelity, and sibling rivalry, their "soulful connection" kept them together.

Carla said that she rarely saw her family. Her father had died three years earlier, and her mother and siblings were scattered throughout the country. The movie was a painful reminder of the lack of soulful connections in her own life. She had friends and colleagues, but like her, they led busy lives, and their crazy schedules prevented them from spending quality time together. Carla longed to be part of a community that shared the same kind of love, commitment, and soul connection she had seen in the movie.

Carla is like every client I've ever worked with. Each one longs for this kind of connection—a soulful feeling that gives them a sense of connectedness and belonging. In the privacy of our coaching sessions, they express a desire to feel seen and heard by others, wanting to know that they matter and that someone is on their side. This is one reason the coaching profession has become so popular. A personal coach fills part of this important need for connection and community.

I suggested to Carla that in an effort to practice extreme self-care, she could create her own "chosen family." By consciously choosing whom to become more intimate with and investing her time and energy into these relationships, she could have the kind of connection she longed for.

Carla agreed, and we created a plan. She would call three friends with whom she enjoyed spending time and ask them to participate in a monthly "dinner club." Each month, one friend would host the others in her home, and they'd each bring a dish as part of a potluck meal. During these monthly meals, Carla would choose a creative, fun way to deepen their relationship and make the evening special.

At the first dinner, Carla brought a board game designed specifically to help the players get to know each other better. Her friends eagerly embraced the idea and enjoyed playing the game. At the next dinner, Carla took several questions from the *IF* book series and typed them on a page. Then she cut the questions out, folded them up, and put them in a jar. After dinner, each woman took turns drawing a question from the jar to answer.

These simple games shifted the conversation among them from a superficial level to a deeper, more personal level, which brought the women closer together. Carla's decision to proactively create a soulful community paid off. All four women looked forward to these monthly dinners and considered them "sacred," rarely missing any throughout the year.

There is a growing hunger for community. This hunger is created by several factors. The information age now offers us the ability to communicate through e-mail and the Internet, making it even easier to be physically out of touch. The workplace, which traditionally provided a sense of community for millions, is also changing. As layoffs and corporate reorganizations continue, employees are motivated to find job security in a new way. Self-employment, subcontract positions, and as *Fast Company*'s cover story of January 1998 labeled it, the new "Free Agent Nation," are turning homes into offices and blurring the lines between work and family. With more people working out of their homes (over fifty million full- and part-time), not only are more Americans working in isolation, but they're working much longer hours. In the end, we wind up being too busy for each other.

In November 1997, the television show *Dateline* polled five hundred people and asked them how they would spend an extra hour of time. Over 75 percent of the respondents answered, "I'd spend more time with loved ones." Life is too short. Our lives are made richer by the relationships that we share with each other. When you come to the end of your life, what will you remember most? Will you want others to know how much money you've made? The successful careers you've had? The education you received? Of course not. You'll want others to know how much you loved them and how much you appreciated the opportunity to share your life with them. You'll want to feel loved and connected in a way that leaves no room for regret.

Stop for a moment and remember a couple of your most special and fondest memories. When you've called them to mind, notice whether these recollections involve people you cared for. Chances are they do. It's the people in our lives who make good times better and difficult ones easier. They enrich our experiences, share our dreams, and pull together the disparate threads that form our personal histories. People, and our relationships with them, are what really complete a whole life.

Unfortunately, because of our busy schedules and daily obligations, we spend much of our time relating to one another on a superficial level. Our busy lives keep us disconnected from each other (even the people we live with), and we miss out on opportunities to experience a soulful connection. By "soulful" I mean the kind of connection that touches your heart and makes you feel grateful for someone's presence in your life. I'm sure you've had the feeling, the one that brings tears to your eyes or makes you smile to yourself as you hang up the phone. It's the lack of this connectedness that makes it easy to take our relationships for granted. You can't miss what you don't have. When we experience the warmth and joy of a deeper connection with others, the desire for community becomes more of a priority. We take the time.

Community makes us whole. It heals us, challenges us to be authentic, and, most important, teaches us to love—ourselves and each other. In the best of worlds, we can turn to those in our community to help us overcome our fear, see the truth about ourselves, and provide the safety and security necessary for us to grow and evolve. Everyone yearns for this in some way. Often this longing is kept secret, as if there were something shameful about wanting and needing love.

If you long for high-quality relationships and deeper connections with others, embrace that desire fully. A loving, supportive community is an integral part of a high-quality life. Many people shy away from taking an active role in community building. They feel it should happen "naturally," the way it "used to." Keep in mind that it's your choice; you can spend your time having dozens of pleasant chats, or you can have meaningful conversations, trustworthy friends, and uplifting relationships. The effort will pay off.

I'd like to help you intentionally build a soulful community. But before we start, let's first look at what makes a high-quality relationship. When you take time for your life and start to experience the joy of living well, you automatically become more concerned with the quality of your relationships rather than the quantity. You feel better about yourself and are less likely to tolerate relationships that drain you or bring you down. Instead, you look for relationships that support you, excite and inspire you, and challenge you to be your best.

As you work through the program in this book and start to change your life, you naturally put yourself into a different category of people—those who are committed to doing whatever it takes to create a life that they love. This can be unsettling to those who feel left in the fast lane or on the outside. But it's extremely important to have a loving community that will support and encourage you as you change your life for the better.

It can be very painful to realize that you've outgrown a relationship. My client Jack experienced this firshand. Jack owns a successful landscaping business. He loves to work outside all summer long, then take off during the winter months. As part of his plan to improve the quality of his life, he set up this business intentionally so that he could take six months off to travel, something he loved to do.

As his business grew more successful, he noticed that some of his friends started teasing him about taking the winter off. They jokingly called him "lazy" and accused him of "goofing off." Jack wasn't amused. He felt put down and made fun of, and when he tried to express his disappointment and frustration, his friends just continued to tease him more. Jack was starting to feel uncomfortable in their company. He couldn't understand why his friends wouldn't support his success.

This is another example of why the coaching profession has grown so rapidly. Although your family and friends love you, they may fear losing the relationship as you make changes in your life. This can result in snide remarks, teasing, being given the cold shoulder, or sometimes outright rude behavior. Be prepared!

What makes a relationship great? How do you know if a relationship is worth investing more time and energy into? To answer these questions, let's take a look at relationships that drain you and relationships that fuel you.

## Relationships That Drain You
Some relationships consistently drain your energy, in both obvious and subtle ways. Several types of people will exhaust you or deter you from your path of extreme self-care. These types include the following:

**THE BLAMER.** This is a person who consistently blames you and/or everyone else for her problems. The world and the people in it always seem to create havoc for this person, and instead of taking responsibility for her life, she'd rather blame others.

**THE COMPLAINER.** This person likes to hear his own voice. He constantly complains about what isn't working in his life and yet never does anything about it. While you're being drained, he actually gets energy from complaining and dumping his frustrations on you.

**THE DRAINER.** This is the needy person who calls to ask for your guidance, support, information, advice, or whatever she needs to feel better in the moment. Because of her neediness, the conversation often revolves around her, and you can almost feel the life being sucked out of you during the conversation.

**THE SHAMER.** This person can be hazardous to your health. The shamer may cut you off, put you down, reprimand you, or make fun of you or your ideas in front of others. He often ignores your boundaries and may try to convince you that his criticism is for your own good. The shamer is the kind of person who makes you question your own sanity before his.

**THE DISCOUNTER.** This is the person who discounts or challenges everything you say. Often, she has a strong need to be right and can find fault with any position. It can be exhausting to have a conversation with the discounter, so eventually you end up giving in and deciding to just listen.

**THE GOSSIP.** This person avoids intimacy by talking about others behind their backs. The gossip gets energy from relaying stories, opinions, and the latest "scoop." By gossiping about others, he creates a lack of safety in his relationships, whether he realizes it or not. After all, if he'll talk about someone else, he'll talk about you. (My colleague Stephen Cluney uses a great technique for dealing with the heated political climate created by gossip at work. He has his clients post a "gossip-free zone" sign on their desks to stop others before they even consider gossiping.)

As you make extreme self-care your standard for living, you'll no longer tolerate these kinds of relationships. Instead, you'll look for people who add to the quality of your life in a positive way—the kind of people who fuel you. Let's look at those types of people.

## Relationships That Fuel You

**PROACTIVE.** This person is on a path of personal development and is proactive in changing her life for the better.

**APPRECIATIVE.** This person consistently appreciates and values your relationship as well as your gifts, talents, and strengths.

**COMMUNICATIVE.** This person is committed to respectful and nondefensive communication, the kind of communicating that brings a relationship closer together instead of further apart.

**ATTENTIVE.** This person pays attention to what you say, withholds judgment, and cares about what you need to feel safe.

**HONEST.** This person is committed to integrity and telling the truth.

**ACCOUNTABLE.** This person takes full responsibility for his part in the relationship and is always willing to look at and deal with how he needs to grow.

## Take Action! Test the Quality of Your Relationships

Since soulful connections require an investment of time and energy, you'll want to choose the people you spend time with wisely. To determine whether a relationship drains you or fuels you, rely on the connection to your Wise Self. Your inner guidance can always be trusted to point you in the right direction. To test this out, choose someone in your community, and as you hold that person in mind, ask yourself the following questions:

*Am I able to be myself with this person? Do I feel accepted by them?*

*Are they critical or judgmental of me?*

*Does the relationship provide an even give-and-take exchange
    of energy?*
*Do I feel upbeat and energized when I'm around this person,
    or depleted and drained?*
*Does this person share my values? My level of integrity?*
*Is this person committed to our relationship?*
*Can this person celebrate my success?*
*Do I feel good about myself when I'm with this person?*

In the best of worlds, our high-quality relationships would be with
people who cared about us, challenged us to be our best, and were
committed to doing whatever it took to make the relationship better.
When you experience this kind of soulful connection, chances are
you'll decide to spend your time and energy on fewer relationships
that run deep rather than too many that exist on a more superficial
level. Choose your company carefully. As you make a point of creating soulful connections, you quickly learn that the richness lies in the
depth of connection. Your Wise Self is your best indicator of the
right relationships for you.

To begin to build a soulful community, I'd like you to take an
inventory of the people who already share your life. This will help
you to identify the people you'd like to go deeper with and the
people you might want to add.

## WHO'S IN YOUR COMMUNITY?

Community lives and breathes all around you. As you consider the
members of your personal community—such as your family, friends,
neighbors, colleagues, and coworkers—expand your thinking to others. People in your local community whom you see on a regular basis
serve as an important part of your life as well. The person who serves
you coffee at your local diner or delivers your mail is part of your
community. The clerk at your local grocery store and the woman at
your local bakery all play a role in your life. Your massage therapist,

hairdresser, doctor, and dentist—these people make up a special kind of community too—a "service" community that not only tends to your personal needs but adds a level of familiarity and belonging that's easily taken for granted.

When my client Paul and his wife moved from California to Florida to be closer to Paul's aging parents, Paul had a hard time adjusting to a new city. All the things he took for granted back home— knowing where the best grocery store or dry cleaner was, having a reliable baby-sitter or trustworthy plumber—suddenly had become major challenges that made him feel uneasy. The simplest tasks, like going to the post office, reminded him that he was a stranger in this new land. This made Paul realize how much he had taken the familiar smiling faces of his local community back home for granted.

My client Vanessa had a similar experience. Every morning before work she stopped at her local bakery for her tea and bagel. For three mornings in a row, she noticed that Lindy, the woman who worked behind the counter, hadn't been there. On the third morning, Vanessa finally asked for Lindy and was disappointed to hear that she had taken another job. Leaving the bakery, Vanessa felt a twinge of sadness. She hadn't realized how much she looked forward to Lindy's smile and upbeat personality until now.

To begin the process of building your community, let's first take an inventory of those people who are already a part of your life. I've listed several categories below to stimulate your thinking. Feel free to adjust the categories to meet your needs. List the individuals who apply to each category.

### Take Action! Take a Community Inventory
My family or chosen family consists of:

_____        _____
_____        _____
_____        _____
_____        _____

The children I love to spend time with are:

_____    _____
_____    _____
_____    _____
_____    _____

The close friends with whom I can share my heart and soul are:

_____    _____
_____    _____
_____    _____
_____    _____

My spiritual community consists of:

_____    _____
_____    _____
_____    _____
_____    _____

My professional community includes:

_____    _____
_____    _____
_____    _____
_____    _____

Acquaintances include:

_____    _____
_____    _____
_____    _____
_____    _____

What about extended family? Would you like to spend more time with members of your extended family? In the process of deepening your community, you may want to get to know your roots before it's too late. This part of your family can offer you a rich and valuable history. Spending time reminiscing and gathering family memories is a key part of a soulful connection. Whom would you like to know better?

-------

My extended family includes (aunts, uncles, cousins, grandparents, etc.):

_____      _____
_____      _____
_____      _____
_____      _____
_____      _____
_____      _____
_____      _____
_____      _____

Other community members include:

_____      _____
_____      _____
_____      _____
_____      _____

As you review the names of people in your community, ask yourself the following questions:

> *Do I have an abundance of community in one area but not in another?*

*Are there people in my community with whom I'd like to*
*connect more deeply?*
*Who's missing?*
*Are there relationships I'd like to have more of?*
*Is there someone I'd like to bring back into my life?*
*Is there anyone I should remove from the list?*

## WHAT'S STOPPING YOU?

Now that you're ready to add to your community, let's take a moment to look at the obstacles that might get in the way. Over the years, I've listened to stories of loneliness and frustration from those who lack the quality relationships they desire. I've also heard the excuses that keep them stuck. There are several reasons why people find it difficult to make new relationships. The common reasons I've heard include these:

*I'm too shy.*
*I'm not sure where to meet new people.*
*I don't know how to meet new people.*
*I feel embarrassed about wanting new friends.*
*I'm too busy.*
*It will take too long to build the history that a good relation-*
*ship needs.*
*I'm too old.*

My client Bonnie longed to have more women friends in her life. We spent a month developing an action plan to help make that happen. But each week during our coaching session, Bonnie revealed that she hadn't made much progress—she couldn't act on the plan. When I asked her what stopped her from taking the necessary actions to make new friends, she explained, "At forty-eight, I shouldn't be needing new friends. Most people have their friendships already in place, and I feel foolish when I think of telling anyone that I want to make new friends. I'm afraid that people will wonder what's wrong with me." Bonnie continued, "It feels too vulnerable to put myself out there. What if no one responds? I hate feeling disappointed, and I certainly don't want to risk feeling rejected."

The last reason is usually the source of the problem. It *is* risky to reach out to others. You may very well be rejected or disappointed. It feels incredibly vulnerable to admit that you'd like to develop new relationships, regardless of your age. But since most of us long for a connection with others, I can assure you that the odds are in your favor. Be willing to risk giving it a try. After all, what have you got to lose—can you imagine a life without soulful connections?

## BUILDING YOUR COMMUNITY

Building a soulful community is a step-by-step, deliberate process to bring certain people into your life. First you decide on the kind of person you'd like to meet (friend, mate, colleague), then you take specific actions to make it happen. I know this may sound a bit calculated, but the truth is that it takes commitment and action to add new people to your community.

When I suggest this process to clients, they usually feel a bit awkward at first. Although the strategy of meeting new people is like any attempt at creating something new, it always feels delicate and strained when people are involved. When I'm speaking to large groups about relationship building, I ask audiences to demonstrate their interest in meeting new people by a show of hands. Usually, at least 95 percent of the hands go up. You're not alone—it's worth the risk. Remember that most people are open, willing, and very interested in making new relationships. And chances are they're just as uncomfortable as you.

Building relationships happens a step at a time, and it will require faith that people will actually show up. If you follow the three-step process outlined below, you're sure to find like-minded people who are anxious to make your acquaintance.

1. Decide whom you'd like to meet.
2. Profile your ideal candidate.
3. Spread the word.

### Take Action! Decide Whom You'd Like to Meet

Review the inventory you completed earlier and look for gaps. Identify the type of relationship you'd like to add to your life. Are you missing close friendships in your life? Would you like to meet a new colleague or find a soulmate? Focus on the kind of relationship you'd like to add. Remember, this is a deliberate plan to bring that person into your life. Focus and intention are key components to building a successful community. Write the type of relationship you want below:

---

### Take Action! Profile Your Ideal Candidate

I know this sounds like some kind of marketing strategy, but the more specific you can be about the kind of person you'd like to meet, the better your chances of attracting that person. Building relationships takes time. If you've ever been on blind dates, you know that you can waste a lot of time and energy meeting new people who do not share your values or interests. Rather than spinning your wheels, why not narrow the field?

Using your journal, make a list of all the qualities you'd like this new person to have. For example, if you'd like to meet a new friend, include the personal interests, hobbies, spiritual beliefs, or intellectual interests that you'd like them to share with you. The more specific you are, the better. If you'd like to meet a soulmate, include the physical characteristics as well. Profile your ideal person. The more focused and clear you are on whom you'd like to attract into your life, the better your chances are of finding someone you'll hit it off with.

Include as many details and characteristics as possible. Your profile may include the following characteristics:

> Physical qualities          Intellectual interests
> Emotional disposition          Hobbies, personal interests
> Spiritual beliefs          Career/financial interests

Over the next seven days, review your list each day and add to it anything that comes to mind. Take your time. By the end of the week you should have a good profile of who this person is.

Next, have someone you respect and knows you well review the list and suggest any missing qualities. This will help make your profile complete.

When you complete your profile at the end of the week, stop and ask yourself an important question: Do I match this profile? Are there qualities on your list that you'll need to develop within yourself in order to participate in this kind of relationship? Like attracts like, and too often we look for relationships (consciously or subconsciously) to provide the qualities that are lacking within ourselves. You may hope for someone who is happily employed because you're unhappy with your job. Or you might insist that someone be able to commit, because on some level, commitment is hard for you. Go through your list and take note of the areas that need your attention. Then get to work on developing yourself. The healthier and happier you are, the healthier and happier your new friend or partner will be.

Let's look at an example of an ideal profile by my client Noreen, a successful painter in her mid-fifties. When Noreen reviewed her community inventory, she felt pleased with the relationships she shared with her family and friends. The missing person in Noreen's life was a soulmate. She wanted to meet someone to share her life with. I asked Noreen to profile her soulmate using the three-step process. When she finished, her list looked like this:

### Noreen's Ideal Soulmate

*Physical Characteristics*

My ideal soulmate will be forty-five to sixty-five years old, five feet six inches or taller, with dark hair and dark eyes. He must be healthy and in good physical shape. I'd like him to feel good about himself, be well groomed, and care about how he dresses.

*Emotional Characteristics*

My ideal soulmate should be emotionally well balanced and committed to doing whatever it takes to be his best. He would be involved in his personal growth by reading, attending workshops, and/or engaging in therapy of some kind. He must be emotionally available for a relationship and excited about making a commitment to someone he loves. He loves the idea of being with a smart, independent, successful woman who needs her space and privacy. He too is independent and enjoys doing things on his own. This man would want to eventually get married.

*Spiritual Characteristics*

My ideal soulmate would be Jewish and actively practicing his faith. He would be interested in sharing his spiritual faith with a partner and is respectful and interested in my spiritual growth as well. He considers himself on a spiritual path and would like to share this journey with a soulmate.

*Personal Interests and Hobbies*

My ideal soulmate loves the outdoors and enjoys activities in all kinds of weather. He likes to walk long distances, enjoys the beach, and has his own hobbies and interests that he'd like to share with me. He would be well read, curious about life, and interested in travel.

*Other Characteristics*

My ideal soulmate is a professional who is financially secure and involved in some kind of work that he loves. He is conservative with his spending habits yet generous and giving in various ways. He has an outlet for expressing his creative interests that he enjoys.

As you can see, Noreen has created an "ideal" partner. Some may say that she's looking for the perfect man. I say, if you're going to put your time, energy, and, most important, your intention and heart into meeting someone to share your life with, make it specific and make it the best.

The chances of Noreen meeting a man who fits this profile exactly may be slim, but by taking the time to think intelligently about what she would like in a partner, and writing it down, she increases dramatically her chances of finding a high-quality relationship. Remember, when you put your intention in writing, you engage a divine power that draws your desire to you. To view this process from another perspective, let's look at my client Jill.

Jill wanted to make new friends. A single mom with one daughter, she was tired of the friends who constantly complained about their lives and never did anything to better their situation. Now that Jill's life was improving, she had to admit that a couple of her friends were not only draining her energy but preventing her from moving forward. Their sarcastic remarks and subtle digs made her question herself, and this was no longer tolerable. Jill wanted new friends who felt good about themselves and who would inspire her to keep growing. Jill's profile looked like this:

### Jill's Ideal Friend

My ideal friend would be a woman with children. She would be content with her life, willing to share herself, and interested in developing a close friendship. This new friend would be physically active, be interested in books and movies, and enjoy family outings with the kids.

Our relationship would be based on honesty and a give-and-take exchange of energy, as well as a desire to help each other grow. She would be thoughtful and caring, and we would be able to talk about anything. It would be great if she were interested in alternative health and gourmet cooking.

Jill's profile was less specific in certain areas but highlighted the important qualities she desired in a friendship. Completing this exercise helped Jill to realize that one of her existing friendships already had the potential to develop into a stronger relationship.

## *Take Action! Spread the Word*

Once you've completed your profile, it's time to share it with others! Let people close to you know that you're interested in meeting this new person, and ask them to introduce you to friends, coworkers, or relatives who come close to your ideal profile. Also, review the acquaintances you listed earlier in your community inventory. Are there people on the periphery of your life who may fit your profile and are just waiting to be invited in? It's not uncommon to review your community and find acquaintances who would make a great new friend or colleague. Sometimes the people we'd most like to meet are staring us in the face.

Put yourself out into the world. Think about the people already in your life with whom you enjoy spending time. How did you meet them? A party, a workshop, or a trip? Create a flyer and hang it in your local library, at the health food store, or on your local chamber of commerce bulletin board. This may sound a bit strange, but it works! The more you're willing to put yourself out there, the quicker the Universe responds.

My client Shelly wanted to add new friendships to her life. She and her husband had one small child and had recently moved to a new city. Shelly wanted to meet other mothers from the community and decided to create a flyer and post it around town. Her flyer looked like this:

### *New Friends Wanted*

Mother of three-year-old daughter, new to the community, seeks other mothers for friendship and shared babysitting. I am a thirty-five-year-old, health-conscious, socially active woman who enjoys reading, cooking, and gardening. I'd love to meet other mothers in the community. Let's have coffee!

Shelly posted this flyer at a local grocery store bulletin board and at an elementary school nearby. She included her name and phone number, and, as a result, five mothers contacted her. Two of them became good friends. Because she was new to the community, Shelly said it gave her a "legitimate" excuse to reach out. Why not try using this idea, if only in your head. What would you do if you were new to your community?

Look for ways to combine meeting new people with doing something that you love. You have a better chance of finding a compatible person by attending programs and events aligned with your values and interests. If you love to sail, why not join a sailing club? If you enjoy mountain biking, why not enter a local race? Attend a workshop or seminar about a topic of interest.

If you're searching for a romantic partner, consider a personal ad. Although it takes time and energy to sort through the responses, I've had several clients and friends who have had great luck meeting people this way. Check out your local newspapers. One of the main local papers in Boston lists not only personal ads of a romantic nature but ads for those people seeking new friendships as well. I've had several clients meet interesting people this way. Other ways to meet people include these:

- *Local Interest Groups*—These organizations are specifically designed to introduce like-minded people to each other. They arrange group theater events, movies, dinners, museum visits, and more. You simply join others at an event that is of interest to you. You can find information about these types of organizations in your local phone book, newspaper community listings, local chamber of commerce, or the back of some local magazines.

- *Adult Education Centers*—Take a class or workshop at your local adult education center. They offer a variety of programs, from flower arranging to meditation classes to wine tasting, that give you the chance to meet like-minded people. Check out continuing education classes at your local universities as well.
- *Volunteer Organizations*—Offer your time, energy, or expertise to a volunteer organization. This provides a great source of community and an easy way to meet great people. Look for organizations that you feel passionate about, and offer your time in ways that allow you to get to know others over time. Don't get stuck working in an office all alone. The goal is to develop relationships while offering your time and energy.
- *Magazines*—Pick up your favorite magazine and turn to the resource section in the back. Check out the listings for events and groups that you can join. You may be surprised to find several listings of events and groups specifically designed to help you meet new people as well.
- *Clubs*—Various clubs focus on special interests. Try hiking, biking, sailing, skiing, or chess. See if you can find a club that will let you try out events before you join. It's a smart idea to get a good feel for a group before you become a member. One of my favorite clubs to recommend is Toastmasters, an international speech club that creates a supportive environment for people who want to learn to speak in public. There are groups all over the world, and it's a great way to meet new people while learning a valuable skill that will boost your confidence dramatically.
- *A Party*—Invite several friends, and ask them to bring along someone new. Pick a theme—a beach party in the middle of winter, a Hollywood costume party at Halloween, or a New England clambake. Sometimes, meeting new people in a group setting can be more comfortable, especially if you have a tendency to be shy.

The process of building a soulful community can be viewed as an adventure. Think of it as a treasure hunt, a magical search for like-minded souls. This way, every encounter has the potential to be a surprise relationship just waiting to happen. Be bold, take risks. The result will be worth it.

## MASTER THE ART OF CONNECTION

As your community develops, you'll have the opportunity to consciously create a more soulful connection with others. Whether with someone new or in an existing relationship, there are specific ways for building intimacy in order to connect with others on a deeper level and create the kind of relationships that enrich your life.

Mastering the art of connection hinges on a willingness to go deeper with others—to be intimate. *Webster's Dictionary* defines intimacy as "closely connected by friendship or association; pertaining to the inmost being." Mastering the art of connection requires a vulnerable act of telling the truth about yourself to share your innermost being with another. Although most of us have not had much training in how to be intimate with one another, chances are you've witnessed our innate human ability to connect in this way.

When faced with a disaster like an earthquake or flood, the inhabitants of cities and towns are known to come together instantly to support each other. People who prior to the disaster had never met rush to risk their lives for their neighbors in distress. This is, I believe, because our basic human instinct is to love and care for each other. In times of pain, we instinctively reach out to offer comfort and support.

A great example of connecting on a soul level was demonstrated by the way people joined together to mourn the loss of Princess Diana. I remember the television filled with images of people embracing and crying together. It was as if the whole world moved in closer to share a common language that lifted our self-conscious barriers.

These kinds of events give us permission to move out of our comfort zones and risk rejection or discomfort. Too often, we wait until it's too late to let someone know how we feel about them. Instead of waiting for a disaster, funeral, or other misfortune to occur, reach out now. By mastering the art of connection, you have an opportunity to create what I call "intentional memories."

Walter, a computer specialist from a large family, was a client who really took to the idea of creating a soulful connection. He wanted to do something to bring his family closer together, and he decided to move outside his comfort zone and take a chance. In the summer of 1997 he and his family gathered over the Labor Day weekend for a reunion. Among his parents, brothers, sisters, nieces, and nephews, there were twenty-two of them staying at the same hotel. On their last evening together, much to his family's surprise, Walter announced that he had created a family game for them to play. Once the children were in bed, they gathered in a circle, nervously awaiting his instructions.

Walter, playing the role of the host, had created a game show. During this show, players were asked trivia questions and received points for each question answered correctly. These questions related to family history, so to answer them each family member would have to recall special memories from their past. As Walter explained the rules, he watched as some of his family members began to fidget in their seats. A couple of people commented on the silliness of a game. Another cracked jokes, but because Walter and I had anticipated this kind of reaction, he was able to take these gestures as a sign that they were struggling with the idea of getting "too close."

Once the game began, they were laughing and yelling and having a grand old time. At the end of the evening, several family members thanked him for investing so much time and energy in creating an evening they'd never forget.

Walter took a conscious risk. By investing his time and energy into creating this game, he risked ridicule and disappointment. But the risk paid off. Without realizing it, Walter had created an "intentional memory," a preplanned event that allowed his family to go deeper and connect on a more soulful level. This memory would stay with each of them for the rest of their lives.

What can you do to consciously create a more soulful connection with the people in your life? To answer this question, travel back to a time when you felt this kind of connection yourself. Using your journal, take a moment to remember the times when you felt connected to someone in your life.

My client Rochelle said that she remembered an incident when a friend had surprised her by coming to the hospital to sit with her while she awaited the results of a test. Although this event took place more than five years ago, she could recall this loving act in an instant.

Jimmy, a client who owned a delivery business, remembered a young girl who had helped him find his lost dog when the dog had wandered away from his delivery truck in the middle of the afternoon. Although Jimmy was a rough and tough sort of guy, he described her loving gesture as something that touched his heart deeply.

Sometimes a soulful connection occurs as a result of simply taking the time to tell someone that you care. These kinds of connections can occur during conversations with our dearest friends, during a meeting with a coworker, or in a brief moment during an exchange with a stranger. When you raise your awareness and take the time to connect with others, every encounter becomes a spiritual engagement.

Let's look at some of the practical ways you can connect more deeply with others. As you read through these examples, pick one and take action now!

## Take Action! Acknowledge and Appreciate Others

How often have you had someone call you out of the blue to tell you how much they appreciated your presence in their life? Or when was the last time someone acknowledged a particular gift, talent, or characteristic that they admired about you? When have you done something like that for someone else? If you're like most people, you probably have a hard time remembering the last time. Taking time to appreciate or acknowledge someone is a great way to deepen a connection. For example, my client Teresa said she was pleasantly surprised by the kind gesture of a coworker who sent her a bouquet of flowers simply to tell her how much he appreciated her support on a project they had recently completed. My client Glen, a professor at a local university, was shocked when a fellow professor distributed a memo acknowledging his "brilliant" contribution to a paper that their department had published. These simple acts of kindness bond people together in very powerful ways that can shift the relationship forever. Let's start with the art of appreciation.

Early in my coaching career, I was taught a powerful exercise by Ed Shea, a relationship coach in Elmhurst, Illinois. Ed has made it his life's work to teach people how to connect on a soul level by using communication techniques based on the work of relationship expert Harville Hendrix. This exercise, called the appreciation exercise, is conducted between any two people (couples, friends, coworkers, business partners, siblings, etc.) who are interested in deepening their relationship and experiencing an overwhelming feeling of love and connection. The exercise uses two statements: "I appreciate you . . ." and "I appreciate me . . ."

To demonstrate how this process works, I've included a sample dialogue between two friends, Jane and Marsha. Jane speaks first by telling Marsha what she appreciates about her, and Marsha responds by mirroring back what she hears. Then Jane shifts her attention and tells Marsha what she appreciates about herself (this is usually the most difficult part). Once again, Marsha mirrors back what she hears. The dialogue goes like this:

*Jane begins by telling Marsha what she appreciates about her:*

> Marsha, I appreciate your no-nonsense approach to handling any problem that comes your way. I also appreciate your sense of humor. You always make me laugh when I really

need it. And Marsha, I really appreciate your thoughtfulness in remembering events that are important to me.

*Marsha acknowledges what she heard by mirroring it back:*

Jane, you appreciate my no-nonsense approach to handling any problem that comes my way, and you also appreciate my sense of humor, which makes you laugh when you really need it. And you appreciate my thoughtfulness in remembering events that are important to you. Did I get that right?

*Jane acknowledges:*

Yes.

*Next, Jane tells Marsha what she appreciates about herself:*

I appreciate my ability to stick with any project until it's completed. I also appreciate the kind of mother I've become and the way I take good care of my children. And I appreciate myself for taking time out of every day to paint.

*Marsha once again mirrors back what she hears:*

So Jane, you appreciate your ability to stick with a project until it's completed. You also appreciate the kind of mother you've become and the way you take good care of your children. And you appreciate yourself for taking time out every day to paint.

*Jane confirms:*

Yes.

Then Marsha would take her turn and Jane would mirror back what she hears. This powerful exercise, which I've used personally in my own life and professionally with clients, may feel a bit awkward at first. But by the time you've finished, I guarantee that you will feel full and deeply appreciated, something we all need more of.

When doing this exercise, feel free to list as many things as you'd like that you appreciate about yourself and each other. Deliver one line, let the other person mirror it back, and then go on to the next. This exercise makes a great ritual for parents and their children, an evening ritual for couples before they go to bed, or a weekly habit for friends who want to keep their connection alive and well.

There are many other ways to appreciate others—sending little notes, making a random phone call, or lending a helping hand. The most important point is to stop and think about whom you appreciate and tell them. If you make it a regular practice, you'll find that you naturally become someone who appreciates others automatically. Stop now and think about whom you'd like to appreciate. List three people here:

1. _____

2. _____

3. _____

Do or say something to express your appreciation this week! Now let's turn to the art of acknowledgment.

To acknowledge someone is to recognize a talent, gift, or characteristic that is unique to them. Instead of acknowledging, most of us have learned to compliment each other. We comment on something we like about another instead of who they are. In other words, compliments are usually about us (e.g., I like your dress, I think you've done a great job on this project, I enjoyed your performance). Using the word "I" is a clue—it's about you.

When you shift your compliments to acknowledgments, by recognizing "who" someone is, you're likely to get a different reaction. My client Brenda decided to practice acknowledging her employees. Instead of the typical "job well done" approach, she started noticing specific contributions and linking them to character traits. For example, her administrative assistant, Jana, was so good at anticipating her needs that Brenda stopped at her desk one morning and said, "Jana, you have such an ability to know what I need before I need it. You are highly intuitive and an important partner in the success of our business."

You'll notice that Brenda used "you" statements instead of "I" statements, so that Jana really felt it was about her and could take it to heart. "I" statements are always about us, whereas "you" statements are about the other person. For example, if you meet a friend for dinner and notice that she looks great, instead of saying, "I really love that outfit," you could say, "You have such a great sense of style and it shows in the clothes you choose to wear." This makes the statement an acknowledgment about her, recognizing her particular talent or gift.

Start to practice this skill with the people closest to you, the relationships that often get taken for granted. Too often, we spend more time expressing our frustrations and disappointments with the ones we love rather than acknowledging who they are and what we love about them.

It's great to practice with children. Why not look for ways to acknowledge who your child is instead of what he does? If you don't have a child, you can practice with a niece, nephew, or the child of a friend. Are they particularly gifted in one area? Tell them by saying, "Margaret, you are so talented when it comes to math, you really have a way with numbers." Or for the son that is particularly creative, you might try, "Matt, you are the most creative kid I know, where do you come up with these great ideas?" Notice how your children respond.

Once again, when you acknowledge who someone is, you're "seeing" them. This creates connection. Why not make it a daily habit—look for someone to acknowledge in the morning, at noon, and again at dinnertime. Not only will you start to automatically look for and acknowledge the inherent talent and gifts in everyone you meet, you'll experience the joy of a deeper connection.

### Take Action! Take Time to "Touch" Someone

I'm a big fan of sending cards and little gifts and leaving funny voice mail messages to brighten someone's day. It's actually a selfish act—I do it because it not only expresses how I feel but makes me smile too! When you "touch" someone by reaching out in a way that is unique and personal to them, a soulful connection occurs. For example, one afternoon in early spring, I was taking a walk along the beach near my home when I came upon a beautiful piece of sea glass. I immediately thought of my sister Michelle and the times we visited the beach together when we were younger. Michelle used to love to pick up sea glass when she was a young girl, so I decided to gather a few pieces and pop them in the mail. Instead of just thinking about her, I wanted to share the experience. I wanted her to share in my fond memory and warm feelings instead of keeping them to myself.

How often have you visited a place that reminds you of someone and recalled a special memory that you shared? Or seen an item in a store that reminds you of someone you care about and thought about picking it up? Why not act on the impulse! Call the person up and share the memory, or purchase the gift and send it as a surprise in the mail. Reaching out to others in this way creates a connection of love that stays with us forever.

Take the time to do the extra things that remind people of how much you care for them. In these days of e-mail and voice mail, it's too easy to feel isolated and disconnected from each other. Why not try some old-fashioned handwriting? Pick someone you care for and send them a handwritten card or letter. How does it feel to you when you receive an unexpected card or note?

Remember birthdays and special events by sending unique little notes or gifts. One of my clients is known for sending little notes that contain seeds that you can plant or little cards that include tea bags. Tell people directly how you feel about them. Have you ever hung up the phone and thought, "Gee, I really like that person," or, "I'm so lucky to have this person in my life"? Why not pick up the phone, call them back, and let them know directly by saying: "You know, Ellen, as I hung up the phone I thought to myself. . . ." Don't keep these thoughts and feelings to yourself anymore. Move them out of your mind and into the world.

Let people know when they've touched you too. When my client Sara was a young girl, her father would tell her that she reminded him of a butterfly because she was such a free spirit. So when Sara saw a crystal butterfly in a store window she immediately thought of her dad. She bought it, wrapped it up, and sent it to him out of the blue. Her father was touched by this gesture. Each time the sun hit it, it sent rainbows of light throughout his office.

Several months later, Sara received a voice mail message early one morning. It was from her father. His message said: "I'm sitting in my office surrounded by rainbows and it made me think of you. I just wanted you to know that I love you—it's your dad." When Sara received the message she smiled to herself and started to cry. Who would have known that such a small gesture would have such a large impact?

How can you "touch" someone today? Choose someone special and list three things that you know are important to them. What do they love? Care about? Enjoy?

*Name*_____

1. _____

2. _____

3. _____

Using one of these items as a theme, do something to show them how much you care. Reach out and "touch" them this week.


### *Take Action! Go on a Treasure Hunt*

Inside each of us lives a multitude of buried treasures—secret dreams, hidden passions, and strong desires that long to be unveiled. One of the best ways to deepen your relationships is to become skilled at the art of uncovering these treasures in others. By asking the right questions, you can enjoy the richness and beauty of everyone you meet.

My best friend, Max, loves people! She is a perfect example of someone who has mastered the art of uncovering hidden treasures. When she walks into a room, she engages everyone with a magnetic quality that invites people to open up and respond. She asks questions, listens intently, and is genuinely interested in the answers she receives. Her questioning is never a "technique"—it comes from the heart and from her natural desire to really know people.

You too can become naturally good at getting to know others on a deeper level by asking questions. For example, asking family members to talk about what they feel grateful for during a Thanksgiving dinner can make the holiday far more meaningful. Holding a dinner party and inviting friends to participate in a "getting to know you better" ritual can make getting to know each other fun. Depending on how close you are, you can use the following questions as a way to connect on a more soulful level:

> *What are you most grateful for?*
> *Was there an event that changed your life? How?*
> *What are you most proud of?*
> *Is there something you wish you could do over?*
> *What are you most afraid of and why?*
> *What was your most embarrassing moment?*
> *Is there something that most people wouldn't know about you?*
> *What have you always wanted to do?*
> *What's the most meaningful experience you've ever had?*

Do what Carla did—invite friends for dinner, put these questions in a hat, and ask each guest to pick one and answer it. When someone is finished answering a question, ask them to choose the next person. At the end of the night, you will have learned more about each other, felt seen and heard, and, I guarantee you, everyone will remember the evening for a very long time. Since our memories are the gifts we carry with us throughout our lives, why not intentionally create them?

You can also use these types of questions in your individual conversations with others. Be willing to go below the superficial level of a chat to a more meaningful conversation. Don't let your own needs get in the way of learning more about others. Put relationships before results. Listen twice as much as you talk, and use the art of asking questions to help you stay focused on the other person—this opens the door for a soulful connection.

### Take Action! Get Back to Basics

One of the simplest ways to create a soulful connection with others is one of the oldest lessons of all—being polite. The simple basics like making eye contact, saying thank you, and being on time are even more important today in our busy world than ever before. These simple behaviors help to support and protect a soul connection between you and the people in your life.

If the eyes are the window to the soul, then it would make sense that you've got to make eye contact to have a soulful connection. Have you ever had a conversation with someone who didn't look you in the eye? While you're doing the talking, they're looking over your shoulder or down at their watch? How does it make you feel? The message that this behavior sends is "You are not important at this moment, something else is." It always amazes me to watch people as they participate in a conversation while looking around the room. It's distracting and rude. Teach yourself to focus on the other person by making eye contact.

Be on time. As you take time for your life, it should be much easier to avoid being late. There is nothing more frustrating than waiting for someone who always abuses your time. Sure, there will be occasions when being late is unavoidable, but with proper planning they should be few and far between.

We've all known people who always arrive late in spite of the frustration and anger it causes. They are the same people whom you ask to arrive thirty minutes earlier than the rest, in the hopes that they'll actually show up. Eventually, being late wears on a relationship, and, although most people will never admit how much it upsets them, you'll find that people just stop inviting you if you're late. Honor your soulful relationships by being on time.

Say thank you. Although most of us learned this skill as children and use it randomly throughout the day, there is a way to say thank you that creates a deeper connection with others and can even create a memorable experience with those you hardly know. It can be as simple as taking someone's hand, looking them in the eye, and saying thank you. Or writing a thoughtful letter letting someone know how their actions or words have impacted your life. Sometimes the best thank you comes as a surprise.

Bring a box of chocolates or homemade cookies to your local post office and thank them for all the service they provide throughout the year. Do this for your local carrier as well. Surprise him or her by leaving a little gift in your mailbox at random times of the year.

Leave an extra $10 tip for the waiter or waitress at your local restaurant who serves you breakfast or coffee each morning. Let them know you appreciate their service. Make an unexpected phone call to someone who provides you with care (massage therapist, hairdresser, or housekeeper) and let them know how much you appreciate their support.

Send a "virtual card," an e-mail greeting, to favorite colleagues and thank them for their partnership. Let them know how much you enjoy working with them. Send a customized gift basket to a client. There are various themes ánd designs to choose from. Send a lobster feast to someone in the Midwest or a pamper basket for the client who has had a baby. Thank someone who doesn't expect it. When my client Jack did this, he was surprised at how the experience touched him.

During a coaching session, I asked Jack to think of those people in his life he felt grateful for. He thought a moment and said that he really appreciated having his yard meticulously cared for by his landscaper, Patrick. I suggested that Jack surprise Patrick with a simple and direct thank you for a job well done.

One day when he came home from work, Jack found Patrick finishing up in the yard. He walked across the lawn, extended his hand, and, looking Patrick in the eyes, said, "You know, Patrick, every night when I come home from work, I look around the yard and enjoy seeing everything so neat and well taken care of. I realize that I never stopped to say thanks. I wanted you to know how much I really appreciate all the hard work that you put into my yard. Thank you."

Patrick smiled shyly and looked down at his feet. When he recovered, he looked up at Jack and said: "Thanks, Jack. Most people never seem to notice." Jack said that the way he felt by Patrick's response made him realize how special and important it is to take the time to thank others. He planned to do a lot more of it!

Whom do you need to notice? Take a few moments and think about those people you'd like to thank. Pick four and write their names here:

1. _____

2. _____

3. _____

4. _____

Now take the time to thank each one in a way that conveys your true appreciation.

———

Imagine what life would be like if we were able to see every meeting with another human being, from the clerk at the local post office to your closest and dearest friend, as a spiritual encounter. Not only would the world be a better place but your life would be made far richer by the hearts that you touch. Too often we seek to fill the void in our lives with "things," and yet real meaning and fulfillment are found in our relationships with each other. Just for today, take time to reach out to someone with the intention of creating a soulful connection.

COACHING REMINDERS
*Don't settle for mediocre relationships—build soulful connections!*

- Be courageous! Don't let the fear of rejection, disappointment, or abandonment stop you from reaching out to others.
- Build your community:
  Decide whom you'd like to add.
  Profile your ideal candidate.
  Spread the word.
- Master the art of connection:
  Acknowledge and appreciate others.
  Take time to "touch" someone.
  Go on a treasure hunt.
  Get back to basics—make eye contact, be on time, say thanks!

## RESOURCES

*GAMES*

**Therapy**
Pessman Toy Corporation

**Game: To Know You Better**
Games Partnership
116 New Montgomery, Suite 500
San Francisco, CA 94105
(800) 776–7662
www.timefortwo.com
  The company has a collection of games for couples that promote positive communication.

**Compatibility**
International Games, Inc. (a Mattel company)
Syosset, NY 11791
  This game helps friends and family to identify ways they think alike.

## BOOKS

**How Not to Stay Single: 10 Steps to a Great Relationship** by Nita Tucker
    and Randi Moret (New York: Crown Trade Paperbacks, 1996)
I recommend this book to any client who is interested in finding a romantic
partner. Relationship expert Nita Tucker presents a unique six-week action
plan for finding that elusive, emotionally fulfilling attachment. This book
teaches readers to stop waiting for a relationship and start making it happen.

**If . . . Questions for the Game of Life** by Evelyn McFarlane, James
    Saywell, David Rosenthal (editor) (New York: Villard Books, 1995)

**If 2: More Questions for the Game of Life** by Evelyn McFarlane and James
    Saywell (New York: Villard Books, 1996)

**If 3: Questions for the Game of Love** by Evelyn McFarlane and James
    Saywell (New York: Villard Books, 1997)

**All About Me** by Philipp Keel (New York: Broadway Books, 1998)
A unique write-in book to help share yourself with others.

**Getting the Love You Want: A Guide for Couples** by Harville Hendrix
    (New York: Perennial Library, 1990)
Another recommendation for every client, this is the bible for healthy and
loving communication. It is an extraordinary practical guide to resolving
problems, using sixteen exercises to enhance communication, stop self-de-
feating behavior, and achieve mutual emotional satisfaction.

**Keeping the Love You Find: A Guide for Singles** by Harville Hendrix (New
    York: Pocket Books, 1993)
Hendrix has developed a brilliant, thought-provoking, innovative self-help
program for single people who yearn for the pleasures and rewards of a
loving, long-lasting union.

*VOLUNTEER ORGANIZATIONS*

**Esalen**
Highway 1
Big Sur, CA 93920
(408) 667–3000

**Omega Institute for Holistic Studies**
260 Lake Drive
Rhinebeck, NY 12572–3212
(914) 266–4444

**New York Open Center**
83 Spring St.
New York, NY 10112
(212) 219–2527

**Mentoring Hotline**
(800) 914–2212

**Big Brothers Big Sisters of America**
http://www.bbbsa.org
   Big Brothers Big Sisters of America, the oldest mentoring organization serving youth in the country, remains the leading expert in our field. BBBSA has provided one-to-one mentoring relationships between adult volunteers and children at risk since 1904.

*OTHER*

**The Letter Exchange**
P.O. Box 6218
Albany, CA 94706
   A place to meet other letter writers by mail.

Send a self-addressed, stamped envelope to:

**Camp SARK**

P.O. Box 330039

San Francisco, CA 94133

> For information on how to start a succulent wild women group (by SARK).

**Ed Shea**

239 East Wilson

Elmhurst, IL 60126

(630) 530–1060

Coachimago@aol.com

> Ed Shea, known as "The Relationship Coach," works with couples and individuals to help them enhance communication and use their relationship as a path toward personal growth and healing. He works nationally with people over the phone.

**Hallmark Connections**

http://www.hallmarkconnections.com

> Great card and gift ideas to say thank you or let someone know you care.

**Card Central**

http://www.cardcentral.net

> Card Central contains hundreds of sites from which to send virtual cards and presents!

**Marliese Designs**

32 Partridge St.

Franklin, MA 02038

(508) 520–4839

> Marliese is a motivational artist who combines words with art to motivate and inspire people. She creates beautiful hand-painted affirmation cards that can be used as gifts and inserts in mailings.

**The Gift Basket**
1500 Main St.
Waltham, MA 02154
(781) 642–1200
www.tgbi.com
> This organization specializes in creating gift baskets for all occasions. It creates theme baskets like golfing baskets, baby baskets, and regional specialties (e.g., New England), occupation baskets (doctors, lawyers, etc.), and food baskets (nuts, chocolate, popcorn, cheese, crackers, candies, cheesecake).

**Green Field Paper Company**
744 G Street
San Diego, CA 92101
(888) 433–6133
> This company offers unique note cards made from recycled products. Its "Grow-a-Note" collection contains seeds so the receiver can actually grow the card, and its "AromaNote" Collection contains the most popular scents of aromatherapy.

**1–800 Flowers**
http://www.1800flowers.com/flowers/welcome
(800) FLOWERS
> Send flowers to someone, or to yourself!

**Toastmasters International**
World Headquarters
23182 Arroyo Vista
Rancho Santa Margarita, CA 92688
(800) 993–7732
> A group of businesspeople who meet regularly to discuss and practice presentation skills. Call to find a local group in your area.

# 7

## Honor

## Your Spiritual

## Well-Being

A book on creating a high-quality life would not be complete without discussing the ways we honor our spiritual well-being. At one point or another, most of us long for more meaning in our lives—a sense of purpose, a connection to something greater than ourselves. This spiritual hunger, like a faint inner voice, remains constant amid the stress of our busy lives, the noise level in our minds, the discontent in our hearts. The voice of the soul calls to us and, although at times we may not hear it, never stops trying to get our attention.

Sometimes clients come to the coaching relationship with a conscious desire to strengthen their ability to hear this inner voice. Other times, clients go through the process outlined in this book and then experience a gradual opening to their inner wisdom, a spiritual awakening of sorts. When this connection is felt, some seek to honor the sacred within a religious context; others take a more nontraditional approach. Once I make the distinction between spiritual and religious to remove any barriers, I make it clear that I've made it my calling to support them in living a life based on their inner truth. After all, every person I've ever worked with has wanted to live a more authentic life, one that reflects who they really are. This to me is a spiritual quest.

When I first began developing my coaching practice, I immediately expected my clients to make their spiritual well-being a priority. I encouraged them to carve time from their busy schedules to meditate, pray, enjoy nature, or do whatever was necessary to connect with their Wise Self and a Divine power. It didn't take long for me to realize that this approach doesn't work. Trying to hear your inner wisdom beneath the roar of a busy life makes living authentically an impossible task.

Most of us struggle to find a way to live authentically in a crazy world. As the poet e.e. cummings once said, "To be nobody but yourself in a world which is doing its best night and day to make you everybody else means to fight the hardest battle which any human being can fight; and never stop fighting." Some of us try to fight this battle by enrolling in meditation classes or retreating to monasteries in search of ourselves, sanity, and the quiet moments that reconnect us to the faint voice of our soul. These methods may work, but they often wind up providing only a temporary solution. Once we're back in the rat race, we quickly lose even the ability to hear our Wise Self, let alone maintain a constant connection to a spiritual way of life. Expecting my clients to create a daily spiritual practice within the context of their busy lives sets them up to fail. So I began instead to help clients eliminate anything that stood in the way of living the spiritual, authentic life they desired.

Now that you've done a great job of creating more time and space in your life and have eliminated many of the blocks, you're ready to develop a practice that allows you to honor your spiritual well-being. In this chapter I'd like to show you how. It would be foolish to think one chapter, or one book, could give you all the tools you need to live each day based on your inner wisdom. The care of your soul is a lifetime journey made up of many twists and turns. That's why I'd like to encourage you to develop a way to honor your spiritual well-being that's personal and unique to you. The culmination of the work you've done so far is an important beginning. The spiritual quest of living an authentic life involves making choices based on your inner wisdom, and this is much easier to do when you have the quiet time and space to hear your Wise Self. You're well on your way.

In this chapter I'll show you how to strengthen the connection to your Wise Self. I'll offer you ideas and tools to develop a personal spiritual practice that fits your life, as well as ways you can nourish and feed your soul to keep the connection open and flowing.

## SPIRITUAL WELL-BEING

What does spiritual well-being mean to you? A sense of oneness with all that is? A relationship with God? A deep feeling of inner peace or the faith to know that everything will always work out for the best?

Sit quietly for a moment and recall a spiritual experience you may have had. When I ask my clients this question, I hear a variety of responses, including these:

> I was walking down the sidewalk toward the Coliseum in Rome. Suddenly, out of the blue, I had a profound sense of being loved and affirmed by God. I don't know where it came from, but it was intense and very real, a feeling of pure ecstasy.

> I was at the symphony, and when I heard the orchestra play a piece by Mozart, I was suddenly moved to tears. I couldn't stop crying. I felt like I was one with the music; it lifted me to a higher place where I felt deeply loved.

> When I watched my son being born, I suddenly understood on a very deep level what real love felt like. I felt myself connected to a force of love that I can't put into

words. All I can say is that it was the most Divine feeling I've ever had.

When I visit my church each week and I sit in silence to pray, I feel connected to God on a very deep level, almost as if God is sitting right there with me, letting me know that everything is alright.

One of the most profoundly spiritual experiences I've ever felt was when I visited Sai Baba in India. This man, this spiritual being, just emanated love. When I watched him walk among the crowd, gently touching the heads of people sitting around him, I felt my heart open.

Although these specific situations differ, there is a common element in every spiritual story I hear—a deep sense of love and connection with a powerful Divine force. It affirms what I believe to be the most profound reason we are here—to learn to love, ourselves and each other. There is no greater calling. There is a common desire shared by people of all faiths to connect more deeply with this divine power of love. And, although our idea of a spiritual life may be different, one thing is clear—the clients who engage in the pursuit of this connection by honoring their spiritual well-being live happier, more fulfilling lives.

In my work as a coach, I've been fortunate to have the experience of feeling this Divine presence during my conversations with clients. There are sacred moments when the truth is told, and a client and I connect on a deep level that opens a door for the Divine power of love to enter. When this happens, I am often moved to tears.

I remember a call with one man in particular. This man worked as an accountant for a large company. Several times over the course of our work together he had shared with me the creative solutions he provided for the problems in his department. One day I decided to tell him how very creative I thought he was. I told him that his ability to solve problems in such an imaginative way was impressive and that he might consider bringing more of this creative talent to other areas of his life.

When I finished speaking, there was silence. I could feel a shift in energy, as though someone reached deep into my chest and touched my heart. My eyes filled with tears, and I hadn't a clue as to why. After a long period of silence, he spoke. This client admitted that he had never thought of himself as creative and upon hearing my words felt overcome with a deep feeling of sadness. No one had ever acknowledged his creative ability before, he said, and for the first time he could remember, he felt "seen," and it touched him deeply. Love was present in that moment, and moments like these serve to remind me that love is the universal spiritual force.

How do you keep this connection alive? What can you do to honor your spiritual well-being, however you choose to define it, in your everyday life?

### THE WISE SELF REVISITED

Thomas Moore defines the soul as the part of us that wants a rich experience of everyday life. This rich experience comes from being in touch with your feelings and your Wise Self and being in constant contact with the Divine. In chapter 1, I asked you to begin awakening the connection with your Wise Self. I suggested that you begin asking for guidance with simple matters, by checking in, writing letters to your Wise Self, and asking for information from your dreams. Then, throughout this book, I've asked you to continue to build on that connection by using your inner wisdom to make practical decisions in your everyday life.

Now I'd like you to take this practice to the next level. If you begin to trust and let go of control, you can actually surrender to a Divine flow of energy that will guide you to your best life—a life you can't even necessarily imagine right now. When the foundation of your life is in good shape (your priorities are straight, you've eliminated what drains you, you're developing financial reserves, etc.), you can begin to let go of setting goals and start to actually live a "goal-less" life. Instead of deciding what you want, you can let Divine guidance direct you to what's next.

### Take Action! Surrender to a Higher Order

The most fundamental way to honor your spiritual well-being and step into the flow is to live a life based on your inner truth—your gut instinct or your Wise Self. If you listen to the wisdom of your soul and take action, you will find yourself headed in a direction that always leads to your highest good. Remember this: practicing extreme self-care will keep the connection to your Wise Self open and available to you. Once you hear the directions, faith and action are the next steps. When all three come together, your highest good will always prevail.

Most of us remember a time when we had a gut instinct or subtle feeling about a direction we should move in. And we all have stories of regret about what happened when we didn't follow the directions. Often, we choose a safer or more familiar path only to discover that our Wise Self held the right choice all along.

I'd like you to remember those times when you were directed by the voice of your soul, your Wise Self, to follow a particular path regardless of what action you chose. Using your journal, recall a time when your Wise Self sent you a direct message about a particular choice to make or direction to take. When did you have a strong gut feeling about something not being in your best interest? When did something feel so right that you knew it was time to move?

Clients will usually acknowledge that they entered into a relationship in spite of knowing on a gut level that it wouldn't work out. Or they just knew it was time to leave a job and, sure enough, once they were gone, the company went under. We all have these stories to tell. Please don't use this as an opportunity to beat yourself up. Use it as a way to acknowledge how often your Wise Self provided you with accurate information. These memories provide wonderful opportunities to remember when your Wise Self has gently (or sometimes not so gently) tugged at your sleeve to steer you in a direction that was for your highest good.

Recalling these events, especially at a time when you're faced with a tough decision, can help you to choose the guidance of your Wise Self even when it seems contrary to what you think is best. First we become aware, aware that the Wise Self exists. Then we learn to tune into that voice, and ultimately we learn to trust it and act on its wisdom. My client Natalie learned this lesson.

Natalie was concerned about money. Although she had reserves set aside in savings, it was the holiday season and her consulting business was slower than usual. During this time she was contacted by a former client who wanted her to take on a large project for a high rate of pay. This project presented two problems. First, it represented the kind of work that she was slowly phasing out of her business; second, although the normal time frame for completing a project of this magnitude was six months, he wanted Natalie to complete it in three.

Natalie's client offered to pay her a handsome fee to meet this deadline, 30 percent more than her normal amount. Given her financial concerns, she considered taking the job in spite of the time frame and nature of the work. She told herself that although she'd have to work weekends, the work would be easy and lucrative.

From the very beginning, however, Natalie said she felt that something was "off." As she discussed the project with this client, she found him to be scattered and unable to provide her with important resources. To complete the project within deadline, it was obvious that she would have to cut corners.

As we discussed her decision, Natalie admitted that her gut instinct told her that this project could be a real problem and that she should decline. She would end up compromising quality and increasing her stress level by dealing with a client whose intentions were suspect. Natalie could tell that taking on this project would not be practicing extreme self-care, but she admitted that she was being seduced by the money. This is where courage and faith come in.

I explained to Natalie that it would take trusting in a Divine presence to make the choice that would honor her well-being. Extreme self-care always comes first. She would be taking a risk by acting on the guidance of her Wise Self, but my experience had shown me that it always pays off. After careful thought, Natalie decided to turn down the project. She called her client and told him that she was unwilling to take on the project because she was committed to providing high-quality service and would have to lower these standards to complete the project within his conditions.

One week later, Natalie received a call about another project. Although this project didn't offer as much money as the prior engagement, it was exactly the kind of work she really wanted to do. In addition, this client was interested in a long-term relationship. This positive experience reinforced Natalie's decision and helped her to trust her gut instinct even more.

Questions about when to leave a job, when to end a relationship, or when to move in a different direction come up all the time. The answer always lies inside. It takes tremendous faith to follow the wisdom of your Wise Self. But the only way to develop faith is by making choices without knowing what the outcome will be. When we act on this wisdom, our lives start to work, we step into the flow, and things seem to magically fall into place.

Start to use the growing connection to your Wise Self in a more proactive way. Get in the habit of asking for guidance on everything. For example, if you have a special dream that you'd like to pursue, ask your Wise Self to show you the next step. Or, if you're unsure about whether to make a change, ask for a sign. When you ask for guidance and remain open to its message, amazing things can happen.

My client Hillary held a secret dream of writing a screenplay. She had a story idea all worked out in her head but had never committed it to paper. Hillary said she didn't know how to begin, and this lack of knowledge made her keep this dream on the back burner. When I asked her to seek the guidance of her Wise Self for the next step, she said that she wasn't even sure that this was something worth pursuing. This is a common response from clients considering action on a secret desire. Resistance is often seen as an easier path than dealing with the fear of failure or disappointment. I asked Hillary to consult her Wise Self anyway, just to see what might happen. She agreed to give it a try.

One month later, Hillary was invited to a dinner party. Sitting next to her during the meal was a man she had never met. As they engaged in a conversation, Hillary was surprised to discover that this man had not only written a screenplay but had recently sold it. She immediately remembered her request for guidance and decided that this was a sign from her Wise Self. Hillary invited the man to lunch, and he agreed to share his knowledge of writing and selling a screen-play with her.

What if you could receive the answers to the most important questions of your life simply by asking? When you make it a regular practice to check in, the guidance starts to flow. A daily spiritual practice is the key that opens this channel to the guidance you desire.

Creating and maintaining a regular spiritual practice is the best way to make your spiritual self-care a priority. By practice, I mean setting aside regular time for those things that honor your spiritual well-being. It might be a daily meditation practice, a walk in nature, or a regular gathering with a spiritual community to share inspiration and insight. Any kind of consistent spiritual activity that nurtures your soul will connect you more deeply to yourself as well as the Divine power that connects us all.

Now that you have more space in your life, it's the perfect time to add or enhance a spiritual practice. The way you honor your soul is a very personal choice—there is no right or wrong way. Make it per-sonal and unique to fit your needs. Before we look at the variety of elements you can use to develop your own spiritual practice, let's look at examples of clients who have developed their own ways of honoring the sacred. As you read about how others care for their souls, pay attention to the elements that feel right to you. Make a note in your journal to use in developing your own practice.

Mark loved the outdoors. He loved to run in the warm weather and ski in the winter months. Mark said that being in nature "fed his soul" and made him feel "more connected to God." When we talked about the best spiritual practice for him, it was clear that Mark needed to do something related to nature. During the warm months, Mark would get up early and go for a run. While running, he'd recite a prayer over and over as a mantra to the beat of his steps. In the winter months, when he was skiing or hiking, he paused often to say a prayer that thanked God for the beauty before him. Mark said he always felt his head clear after this time in nature. Now, when he feels stuck about a particular direction or choice, he goes out into nature to ponder his options. This has become his way to commune with the Divine.

Jason, on the other hand, decided to make meditation his daily practice. He created a space in his living room where he placed candles, incense, and several favorite items that had special spiritual meaning for him. Jason visited this sacred space each morning before going to work and again in the evening when he came home. He focused less on how much time he spent there and more on the quality of his experience. In the morning, he'd begin his ritual by reading an inspirational passage from a favorite book. Then he'd light a candle, close his eyes, and sit in silence for as long as he felt moved to. When he returned from work in the late afternoon, he gathered his mail, changed his clothes, and went back to sit again. Jason imagined clear, clean energy coming into his body with each inhale and all the day's tensions pouring out of his body with each exhale. As months went by, the amount of time he spent in meditation increased.

Deirdre worked in a big city. She often complained of how hectic and frenzied the energy felt on her way to and from work. I challenged her to find a creative way to use her subway ride as a spiritual practice. Deirdre met my challenge by deciding to sit quietly and send her fellow passengers love. Slowly, she'd look around at the people sharing her car, smile, and say quietly to herself: "I send you love, I send you love." This simple practice transformed a morning frustration into a peaceful discipline that set her day off right.

Marty was in great shape. He loved to work out and found a

perfect way to honor his spiritual well-being. Each time he went to the gym, Marty used his weight training as a form of meditation. He would raise and lower the weights slowly, imagining a powerful inner force building inside him. He focused intently on strengthening this inner connection while strengthening his body. Not only did Marty feel physically rejuvenated when he left the gym, he felt spiritually rejuvenated as well.

Marla loved to dance. She had a large space in her home where she danced almost every day. She said it lifted her spirits and made her feel connected to the Universe. Marla decided to use her love of dance as part of her spiritual practice. She had read that ancient cultures used dance and song to worship their Gods. They would offer their dance up to the Gods as a form of prayer. This sounded to Marla like a perfect way to combine the two. Each time she started to dance, she recited a prayer of offering to the Universe.

Each of these clients found a personal and unique way to honor their spiritual well-being. You can too! Let's design yours.

## Take Action! Design Your Spiritual Practice

How will you honor your spiritual well-being on a regular basis? Where will you connect with your Wise Self, God, or a Divine presence? To design your spiritual practice, we'll look at the best place, time, and method for you to personally honor your spiritual well-being.

CREATE SACRED SPACE. Creating sacred space to honor your spiritual well-being means deciding on an actual location, the best time of day, and the right frequency for you. Most people think of a spiritual practice as a daily event done in solitude. But as we've seen from the examples above, it can be something quite different. Let's start by considering the place.

You may want to find a place in your home that you can set aside for spiritual rejuvenation. It may be the corner of a room or a whole room. Find a space that looks, feels, and smells right to you. Clean the area well—vacuum, dust, polish, whatever it takes to have the spot feel fresh and clear. Next, check the lighting. Is it appropriate day or night for your optimum comfort? Then, gather any items that may help make it a sacred space for you. The items might include sage or incense, pictures, candles, symbols, books, pillows, blankets, flowers, or statues. Gather things that you love and place them in this space.

Now, sit in the space and notice how you feel. Does the energy feel peaceful? Is it quiet enough? You want to experience an overall sense of peace and mindfulness when visiting this place. Make the necessary adjustments. Over time, you can adjust this space as your needs change. Have it be a place that calls to you, a place that you look forward to spending time in.

You may decide that a place outside your home feels better for you. Is there a favorite place in nature that you like to visit? A lake, the seashore, or a park? My client Louise has a special spot in a local park that she loves to visit on her way home from work. The park looks out over a pond, and she sits quietly and just stares into the water.

Notice the places that feed your soul, and spend more time there. Enjoy an ocean walk, a hike through the mountains, the fall foliage or a summer sky. Imagine that they are meant just for you, to feed your soul.

Many people find the quiet and peace they long for in more traditional places of worship. A local church or temple may be the perfect place for you to commune with the Divine. If you haven't been to a church or synagogue for a while, go back and visit. My clients Phil and Georgia were surprised to find that the Sunday services of their local Unitarian church included spiritual readings from some of their favorite authors, like Matthew Fox and Marianne Williamson. They were excited to find a new spiritual community.

You may choose a variety of places. There are no rules. You may develop a daily practice in your home and go to church each week.

Or spend time in nature during the warm weather and move into your home when it gets cold. Remember, it's what works best for you. Write your sacred places here:

_____

_____

**CHOOSE THE BEST TIME.** Finding the right time to set aside for your spiritual practice is an important factor in creating a consistent practice. For those who like a daily practice, the early morning might be a great way to start the day. For others, practicing in the late afternoon or evening may be better as a way to complete the day. How frequent do you want to practice this discipline? Every day? Once a week? Once a month? Choose a time frame that you'll easily be able to commit to. Don't set yourself up to fail. Although I recommend a consistent daily practice, start slow and build on success. Honoring your spiritual well-being consistently will make you feel better about yourself. Write your best time(s) here:

_____

_____

**CHOOSE YOUR PERSONAL SPIRITUAL PRACTICE.** What you decide to do as a spiritual discipline or practice is strictly a personal choice. Use some of the examples listed earlier in this chapter to experiment. Try different approaches until you settle into one or more that feels right to you. You may choose to listen to spiritual music, light a candle and quietly pray, or study a passage from the Bible or other spiritual teachings.

You may decide that an important way to honor the sacred is by sharing your spiritual journey with others. Creating a sacred circle of friends, where it's safe to share your vulnerable self, might be the perfect addition to your spiritual practice. My client LeAnn found this to be a very important element.

LeAnn gathered several friends who shared her desire to bring more of the sacred into their everyday lives. They agreed to meet once a month to share the various ways that they each honored their souls. Sometimes, one member would share inspirational readings, another might bring specific questions to prompt a group discussion, and other times they found themselves sharing "miracle stories," the synchronistic events that appeared to most to be just coincidences. LeAnn looked forward to these gatherings and said that they not only deepened her spiritual awareness but gave her a chance to hear the wisdom of God through others. It was the perfect way to honor her spiritual well-being. Two years later, this monthly gathering is still going strong and has become an important part of LeAnn's life.

Who are the people in your life with whom you can share your spirituality? Do you have a spiritual community? Would a regular meeting be a rich, soul-honoring experience for you? We all need a personal spiritual community to encourage us to explore our spiritual natures more fully. Traditionally, our spiritual communities have been found in churches and temples. Although many still find these to be fitting places, many clients complain about a lack of connection with the people who share their place of worship. Reach out to fellow members. Offer to start a group yourself. Find people with whom you feel safe, who will not judge your spiritual beliefs and practices. Think of the people in your community you might like to share your spiritual practice with. Write their names below:

_____     _____
_____     _____
_____     _____

Your journal can also become a trusted spiritual guide. Use it to explore your thoughts, feelings, and spiritual desires. Write your own prayers. Keep track of your favorite spiritual quotes, memories, synchronistic events. Capture them in your journal and revisit them for inspiration. Let journal writing become part of your spiritual practice.

When I was reawakening my spiritual life after drifting away from my Catholic upbringing, I spent a year writing letters to God every day in my journal. I longed to reconnect with a power greater than myself and spontaneously started this daily ritual. Each day built on the one before, and this practice did in fact reconnect me with God. My journal became a companion on my spiritual journey.

Try it for yourself. Take out your journal and write a letter to God, the Universe, Jesus, Buddha, your Creator, the Great Spirit, or the Divine—whatever spiritual relationship feels comfortable to you. Write a letter each day for one week. Imagine that a great power is listening to your every word.

Look for ways to incorporate other rituals into your daily life. The intentional use of rituals can be a powerful reminder to hold ordinary events as sacred. The simple act of blessing a meal, burning incense while reading a book, or lighting a candle while you work can add a sacred quality to everyday life.

Now that you have plenty of ideas to choose from, write the ones that feel right to you. Ways to honor my spiritual well-being:

_____

_____

_____


Now let's put it all together:

My sacred place(s) will be:

_____


The best time for this practice is:

_____


My spiritual practice consists of:

_____

### Take Action! Feed and Nurture Your Soul

What moves you? What feeds your soul and makes you feel deeply? Is it great music, a spectacular sunset, or ecstatic dance? Or maybe it's those moments when things just seem to come together, and you feel overwhelmed with gratitude. Pay attention to the things that give you chills, the positive experiences that make the hair on the back of your neck stand up or move you to tears. Write these things down. These are the things that feed your soul.

We all need "soul food." When we feed our souls, we open ourselves to the experience of grace—a moment when time stands still and we can feel a Divine presence enter our hearts and minds.

Soul food can move you physically and emotionally, as well as spiritually. My client Toby remembered attending a conference that opened with several drummers on stage. The loud, rhythmic beat had her up and off her seat in no time. She said she felt a primitive presence take over her body. My client Andrew had a similar experience at the theater. He went to see *Les Misérables* with his wife and was mesmerized from beginning to end. Andrew said that the performance stirred some force deep within him. These are the kinds of events that we often save for special occasions. But our souls need to be fed more than once or twice a year. I'm now giving you permission to feed yourself hearty soul food on a regular basis to protect your spiritual health!

CREATE AMAZING MOMENTS. Some of the best ways to feed your soul are with what I call "amazing moments." We create amazing moments by taking risks and doing those things that we love that might be outside our comfort zone. While flying back from New York once, I came upon a story of amazing moments in an in-flight magazine.

The journalist, Bob Spitz, had attended a rock-and-roll fantasy camp for people who held a secret dream of playing music onstage with a favorite, famous musician. At this camp, men and women of various ages gathered to spend several days fulfilling their dream. Spitz recalled their childlike excitement at the thought of playing alongside their aging idols. There were several amazing moments, one of which involved Waldman, a middle-aged management consultant from Pennsylvania. Spitz wrote: "Waldman was playing on stage with Nils Lofgren, enjoying a simple jam of blues, when Lofgren yelled, 'Take it!' Waldman froze, then yelled, 'NO!' He said that he was terrified for a second or two but afterward, when he went back to his room, he looked in the mirror and yelled, 'THAT WAS THE MOST AMAZING MOMENT OF MY LIFE!' " Soul food? I think so.

I remember an experience that served as an amazing moment for myself and seventy other women. I'd been asked to present a workshop at a women's conference for a local university. During this workshop, I asked each woman in the audience to write down a goal she wanted to accomplish and a list of what she believed was preventing her from achieving this goal. I then asked for a volunteer willing to share her goal and obstacles with the group. Sandra was sitting in the second row and quickly raised her hand.

She walked to the front of the room and stood nervously before the group of women. She announced that her goal was to play the piano in front of an audience—although she was a well-trained classical pianist, she suffered from severe stage fright, her obstacle. Sandra desperately wanted to play in front of people once again.

I began questioning Sandra about her stage fright. As she talked about the symptoms, I listened carefully for the source of her fear. As a young girl, Sandra had been forced to play the piano for friends and relatives. She felt pressured to "perform" and became anxious about making mistakes. Her fear became so intense that, when she got older, she decided to stop playing for others completely. The closest Sandra had come to performing for anyone was to open a window while playing at home, knowing that others might walk by. She had not played in front of anyone for more than twelve years.

I explained to Sandra that as an adult she now had a choice of whether or not to play. I went on further to point out that by not overcoming this fear, she might actually be holding herself back from other choices that could dramatically improve her life.

I remembered that there was a piano outside the room at the end of the hall and, using a paradoxical approach, I asked Sandra if she'd be willing to play a one-minute piece for us, *with* mistakes. All at once the women jumped to their feet to show Sandra their support by giving her a standing ovation.

After a break and much deliberation, Sandra decided to accept my challenge. At the end of the workshop, we filed into the lobby, where the piano stood against a wall at the end of the hall. As we gathered around her, Sandra gently sat on the bench. Then, after a long pause and a deep breath, she proceeded to play the most beautiful classical piece I'd ever heard. Time stood still. Her willingness to be vulnerable in front of these women opened the door for a Divine presence to enter, a presence so strong that many of us were instantly moved to tears. Deeply touched by her courage, I knew we would always remember this moment and our lives would be changed forever. That's what soul food does.

This event happened over five years ago. Imagine my surprise when, out of the blue, I received a phone call from Sandra while writing this book. She said that she happened to be thinking about this event and decided to call and let me know that the experience we shared was still impacting her life today. Anytime she was faced with a choice that required courage, she reached back in time and called upon the love and support of every woman in that room.

The events and experiences that feed your soul hold within them a fuel that is carried throughout a lifetime. And, like Sandra, you can call upon this power to fuel you in your present-day life.

How will you create amazing moments? What have you always dreamed of doing but felt too afraid to try? Move outside your comfort zone and feed your soul! Use your coaching partner or group to discuss ways that you might create amazing moments together.

INDULGE IN ''VISUAL SOUL FOOD.'' Some of the best soul food is just outside your window—a spectacular sunset or sunrise, a hike up a mountain overlooking the splendor of the land, a full moon, or the chance to lie on your back and watch the stars. This is what I call visual soul food, and this kind of food is free and abundant. Where can you go to feed your soul? Is there a special garden, butterfly farm, or bird sanctuary? List three places here:

1.  _____
2.  _____
3.  _____

**NURTURE YOUR SOUL WITH THE "LITTLE THINGS."** Sometimes we nurture our soul with the little things, the kinds of things that we didn't have time for when we were too busy—things like painting your nails, weeding a garden, filling a bird feeder, or sharing afternoon tea with a friend. These may seem like strange examples of soul food, but you'd be surprised at how many people long for the opportunity to enjoy these simple things.

Give yourself the gift of an afternoon or day just to do the little things that bring you joy. As you go about your week, make a note of the little things you'd like to do, then list five examples here:

1.  _____
2.  _____
3.  _____
4.  _____
5.  _____

Someone once said that the senses are the gateway to the soul. Sensual things will feed and nurture your soul too. Make love to powerful music, sleep on Egyptian cotton sheets, or wear silk or velvet next to your skin. Drink tea from a fine antique teacup, or travel with silk pillowcases. Light candles during the day, or fill your room with the sensuous smells of aromatherapy. Engage in deep, spiritual conversations with others to share those things that feed your soul.

Using suggestions from this chapter as well as your own, what will you do to feed your soul? List ten examples here:

1. _____

2. _____

3. _____

4. _____

5. _____

6. _____

7. _____

8. _____

9. _____

10. _____

Now make a commitment to do one a week. Which one will you do first?

_____

When?

_____

### Take Action! Plan a Regular "Retreat for Your Soul"

To make the care of your spiritual well-being a priority, take time out regularly for a soul retreat. How many times have you wished that you could take time off to reconsider your life in some way? A sabbatical from the daily obligations that would allow you to regroup and assess a particular situation or even the direction of your life? This "retreat for the soul" is a requirement for creating the life you want. Life changes, people change, and circumstances change—we all need this time for quiet and contemplation on a regular basis.

Some people use a yearly event as a time to take a soul retreat. Each year, my client Elaine uses her birthday as a sacred time to reevaluate her life. She plans a three-day visit to a monastery or quiet retreat and submerges herself in silence. She reviews the events of the prior year and writes about how she's grown from the experiences. Then she plans the next year. She makes a list of the ten things she'd most like to see happen. Included in this planning are the qualities she'd like to develop in herself and the ways she'd like to grow personally. This yearly ritual has become a sacred event that Elaine calls "the greatest birthday gift of all."

Another client, Ellen, uses the winter and summer solstices as her reminder that it's time to take a retreat for her soul. She plans a trip to a spa, where she's pampered and has a chance to focus "soul-ly" on herself. Ellen arrives back to her life rejuvenated and refreshed, ready to make any necessary changes to keep her on the right track with the direction of her life.

Your retreat may be something altogether different. How about a whitewater rafting trip? Or a biking excursion? Some clients enjoy a vision quest of sorts, where they spend time in nature and may even challenge themselves to reach beyond their normal limits.

Time for soul searching is a must to maintain a high-quality life. It's a perfect opportunity to reevaluate your spiritual practice, gain insight and guidance from your Wise Self, and reevaluate the way you're living your life. Time away provides perspective. Too many times, clients tell me that they dream of a chance to take a sabbatical, a time away from it all just for them. I say build it in, make it a priority—stop dreaming and start planning!

So, when will you schedule your first retreat? Fill in the blanks below:

My first "retreat for the soul" will be scheduled for:

_____

To take this trip, I must:

_____

The number of days I'd like to take are:

_____

The place I'd most like to go is:

_____

I'd like to use this retreat to:

_____

The three action steps I need to take first are:

_____

_____

_____

If taking a retreat for the soul feels impossible, use your coaching partner or group for support. Ask them to help you uncover what's standing in your way, and have them brainstorm ways to help make it happen. If money is the issue, go back and revisit chapter 4. You can also check out the resource section at the end of this chapter for low-cost retreat and sabbatical options. If you find yourself saying that you don't have time, go back to chapter 2 and get cracking!

———

When you live your life based on your inner wisdom, your Wise Self, you come to realize that the life you thought you wanted was only the beginning. A Divine power takes over, and as you listen to and act on your inner wisdom, you're guided to a life beyond your wildest dreams. Now that you've put a spiritual practice in place that allows you to feed and nurture your soul, make it your number one

priority! Let the connection to your Wise Self become your primary
fuel in life!

## COACHING REMINDERS
*Surrender to a higher order—trust your gut and let your Wise Self guide you.*

- Design a unique and special spiritual practice that works for
  you.
- Feed and nurture your soul:
    Create amazing moments.
    Indulge in "visual soul food."
    Nurture your soul with the little things.
- Plan a regular "retreat for the soul."

# RESOURCES

*MAGAZINE*

**New Age Magazine**
P.O. Box 488
Mt. Morris, IL 61054–8244
(815) 734–5808
$12/one-year subscription

*BOOKS*

**Sanctuaries: The Complete United States: A Guide to Lodgings in Monasteries, Abbeys, and Retreats** by Jack Kelly and Marcia Kelly (New York: Bell Tower, 1996)
This book features wonderful low-cost places throughout the United States that welcome people of every denomination. Most are Christian, but many are Buddhist, Sufi, and Hindu, and a few are without specific religious ties.

**Creating Sacred Space with Feng Shui: Learn the Art of Space Clearing and Bring New Energy into Your Life** by Karen Kingston (New York: Broadway Books, 1997)
This easy-to-understand, illustrated guide shows how to apply the art of space clearing and other principles of feng shui to create inner peace and comfort in the home and workplace.

**Illuminata: A Return to Prayer** by Marianne Williamson (New York: Random House, 1994)
A beautiful book filled with rich prayer and wisdom that encourages the reader to "look to God" to deliver us from the pain of living.

**Many Lives, Many Masters** by Brian L. Weiss (New York: Fireside Books, 1989)
This book takes readers on a unique spiritual journey that will change their lives.

*Celestine Prophecy* by James Redfield (New York: Warner Books, 1993)
This spiritual adventure contains vital lessons in the form of nine insights
that put the reader on a path toward a completely spiritual culture on earth.

*Living in the Light: A Guide to Personal and Planetary Transformation* by
       Shakti Gawain (New York: Bantam, 1993)
One of the original, best books for developing your intuition and learning
to follow it.

*Sermon on the Mount* by Emmet Fox (HarperSanFrancisco, 1989)
This book offers practical guidelines to people of all faiths who seek to
bring health, happiness, and true prosperity into their lives and the lives of
others.

*Six Months Off: How to Plan, Negotiate, and Take the Break You Need
       without Burning Bridges or Going Broke* by Hope Dlugozima, James
       Scott, and David Sharp (New York: Henry Holt, 1996)
A take-action how-to book on how to plan for a sabbatical or time off from
work.

*Awakening the Buddha Within* by Lama Surya Das (New York: Broadway
       Books, 1997)
Written by the most highly trained American lama in the Tibetan tradition,
this book is accessible and compelling to the modern-day spiritual seeker.

## OTHER

**Rock and Roll Fantasy Camp**
252 West 71st Street
New York, NY 10023
(212) 757–1605

# 8

---

# Your

# New

# Life

---

You have set in motion a new way of living. By turning the seven obstacles into stepping-stones, you have given yourself a choice about how you live your life. Not only has the quality of your outer life improved dramatically, but you should notice the quality of your inner life improving as well. As you spend your time and energy on what really matters and enjoy the fruits of your labor—such as increased financial security and the joy of soulful connections—your confidence will increase, peace of mind will take over, and you'll feel empowered to live life on your terms.

By taking full responsibility for your life, you have found the key to true security—the kind of security that comes from having abundance in all areas of your life: time, energy, community, and spiritual well-being. You'll find yourself saying the kinds of things I hear clients say:

*I have more than enough time to do the things I want to do.*
*I feel relaxed and peaceful most of the time.*
*I'm enjoying quality time with family and friends.*
*My friends and family tell me that I'm easier to be around.*
*I have fewer conflicts and frustrations in my life.*
*I wake most mornings with a smile on my face.*
*My physical health has improved.*
*I feel more secure about money.*
*My home and office are a joy to be in.*
*I feel hopeful and excited about my life.*
*Great opportunities seem to magically come my way.*

These are the signs that your hard work is paying off. Continuing the process outlined in this book is your insurance policy for a life of extreme self-care. If you find yourself getting caught up in the rat race again or feeling overwhelmed or frustrated with your life, simply ask yourself the following questions to determine where you need to get back on track:

### Quality of Life Checklist

1. Am I taking extremely good care of myself? Do I take time out of my schedule *every* week just for me? (chapter 1)
2. Have I updated my Absolute Yes list in the last three to six months, and does my schedule reflect these priorities? (chapter 2)
3. Am I tolerating any person, place, or thing that is draining my energy? (chapter 3)
4. Am I living within my means, saving consistently, and investing wisely? (chapter 4)
5. Am I fueling my body, mind, and spirit with premium sources of fuel? (chapter 5)
6. Am I strengthening my soulful connections with the important relationships in my life? (chapter 6)
7. Am I consistent with my spiritual practice, listening to and

acting on the wisdom of my Wise Self and a Divine power? (chapter 7)

Change is constant, and you'll need to revisit the program in this book from time to time to continue creating the life you want. Use the Quality of Life checklist to identify where you need to refocus your energy, and go back to the corresponding chapter and get to work! Each time you do the exercises, you continue to build on the work you've already accomplished.

## REINVENTING HOW WE WORK

Now that you have refocused the vision for your whole life and built a strong foundation for your new life, you're in a much better position to think differently about your work. It's time to ask yourself how work can actually add value to your life.

As you've gone through the program in this book, reclaimed your personal power, and taken charge of your life, you naturally started to live a more balanced life. Your life stopped revolving around your work, and the focus of your energy shifted to include your relationships, your spiritual life, and fun in addition to work.

As my clients go through the process outlined in this book, they feel empowered to make changes in their work lives. Once they've begun to think of their lives as an unlimited canvas, they give themselves creative license to paint their dreams. To do that, some of them decide to change the kind of work they do, while others change how they do it. Either way, the goal is to have work add a dimension of richness to your *whole* life.

For example, some clients decide to stay at their present job and improve their work environment. Others leave to start their own businesses. And some even customize their work to not only fit their new life but to express their passions and desires. Let me give you some specific examples of what I mean.

My client Timothy loved his work as a software engineer and was happy with the company he worked for, but when he set new priorities, he realized that spending more time with his children while they were growing up was very important to him. Unfortunately, his company's culture rewarded employees for working long hours, and, feeling the pressure to conform, Timothy felt compelled to stay at the office beyond 6 P.M.

Once our coaching got started and Timothy began getting his life in shape, he applied what he had used so successfully in his personal life to improve his job. Timothy set new priorities at work, made sure he spent his time and energy on these priorities, eliminated the things that were draining his energy, and rallied his coworkers and staff to support these new goals. After six months, his boss began commenting on the changes he noticed, from the new look of Timothy's organized office to the projects that consistently got completed before deadlines.

Taking advantage of this new reputation, Timothy and I devised a plan that would allow him to work at home two days a week to see his kids when they got in from school. The plan included specific objectives to be met and described the kind of work that he could do more effectively without interruptions at home. He pointed out the potential pitfalls, provided solutions, and asked his boss to give it a try for thirty days.

I suggested that Timothy approach his boss from a partnership perspective, letting him know that he was committed to *their* success. I helped him to put the goal, the plan, and the successful outcome he imagined in writing; this way, he could practice not only what he would say but how he would say it. When Timothy explained the importance of being with his children and presented his boss with a well-thought-out plan in a straightforward, confident way, his boss agreed to give it a try. At the end of thirty days, after making some adjustments, Timothy and his boss concluded that this new way of working made sense.

Timothy could afford to take the risk of alerting his boss to his changing needs because he had proven his ability to work smart. Also, because he had the emotional and financial reserves, he felt secure knowing that he could choose to leave the company if this arrangement didn't work out.

Remember, with a strong foundation in place, you take back your power and put yourself in charge of your work life. It's up to you to take full responsibility for what isn't working and change it. No one else will do that for you. Instead of feeling like a victim of circumstance, you can speak up, say what you want, request a change, and have your work life add value to your whole life.

When my client Stacy was well into the coaching process, she decided to take a different route. Stacy left a position in the travel industry to start her own business. Drawing on a hunch that people could work together from a distance, she created an office in her home and started to assist business owners "virtually." Not only did she handle their travel, but she conducted research, helped make important business decisions, and provided all kinds of administrative support. With six months worth of living expenses as a cushion and two clients already lined up, she launched a successful business. At the end of the first year, she had more clients than she could handle and decided to expand her success by creating a "virtual training company" that would train others in this new art of "virtual assisting."

Stacy not only enjoys the freedom and independence of working for herself, but she reaps the financial rewards as well. Like so many other home-based business owners, Stacy now earns three times what she did working for someone else. Feeling empowered in her own life, she has designed a company that empowers others by giving them the tools to create work that supports their lives. For example, a majority of Stacy's clients are women who can now build a lucrative business that allows them to stay at home while raising their children.

And, as is typical, once Stacy got her life in order and felt better able to make the choice to have her work life add value to her personal life, everything seemed to fall into place. Within six months of launching her company, Stacy was featured in three major magazines, and her business took off. Luck? No. Hard work, a solid foundation, and the support of friends, family, and a Divine force—the magic that's available to us all when we commit to living a high-quality life.

Sometimes a client who already has a business in place decides to make a change. More and more of the business owners I work with are realizing that bigger is not necessarily better. With added success comes added responsibility. As the business grows, the owner is forced to develop a whole new set of skills. Like my client Christine, some decide to jump ship midstream and give up the fast pace of business growth for a slower, more personally rewarding one.

Christine has a passion for travel and photography. From the moment we met, she talked about the various places she had visited and the joy she felt while taking pictures of each one. Her love of travel and photography has now become an integral part of her holistic life. Christine was a very successful corporate consultant who used to work seventy hours a week, but now that she's customized her livelihood, she has taken her business to a new level. Christine now takes on only three corporate projects a year; by doing this, she has freed up more than four months to travel.

As Christine went through the process outlined in this book, she realized that her desire to travel and her love of photography far outweighed her desire to be wealthy. She now rents a modest studio apartment, lives well within her means, saves 50 percent of her consulting income, and uses the rest to pay for her trips. And that was only the beginning. Once again, Christine's story really captures the magic that occurs when we're not only doing work we love but, more important, living a life we love.

Two years into this new way of life, Christine was sharing photos of a recent trip to Ireland with a corporate client. The client was so moved by the way she captured the essence of the people and the land that she contacted her a week later and asked her to meet for coffee. As soon as they sat down, this client asked Christine if she would be interested in doing a travel/photo expedition for their next product launch—a global software program billed as the "eyes of the world." This project would send Christine around the world for the next six months taking pictures of various cultures. Needless to say, Christine was thrilled!

These examples are typical of what happens when clients go through the program in this book and decide to do work on their own terms. Most people never get the chance to experience this kind of choice and Divine support because they're too busy struggling to survive. But now *you* get to call the shots. You've earned the right to decide not only what you'll do but how you'll do it. You've given yourself permission to play by a new set of rules.

Success is a given for clients who work hard to build a strong foundation for their lives. And, the truth is, these same clients make the best employees and business owners. By improving their lives, they've learned important skills that build professional success as well.

So, for those of you who are looking for the best, listen up! Once they've reached the point when they feel secure enough to choose their work wisely, my clients demand more than a good paycheck from their job. The following criteria must be met:

- Work must never cause them to compromise their integrity.
- The required hours must allow them to have a life outside work.
- Their contribution must be acknowledged and appreciated.
- Their work must be challenging and fulfilling.
- They must have an opportunity to use their best talents and gifts fully.
- They must be able to provide their input for important decisions.
- Their work must serve a greater purpose.
- They must be paid fairly for the work they perform.

When these pieces are in place, employees and business owners alike feel compelled to succeed. It becomes a win/win situation for employers, customers, and clients, as well as coworkers. Congratulations!

You've earned the right to be choosy and to do the work you love that supports your whole life.


## DOING WORK YOU LOVE

Most people live their lives unaware of or holding onto a secret dream or desire that never sees the light of day. Either they're too afraid to admit what is most dear to their heart, or their lives are so filled with clutter that they can't yet see the hidden gifts that they have to offer.

I believe that every person has special talents and gifts to share with the world. But, contrary to popular opinion, I also believe that these gifts and talents go undiscovered or underutilized because there is not enough focus and attention on the quality of our lives. Countless times I've heard the frustration that comes with not knowing what you love or not being able to do it. I usually start the conversation by sharing the following old, favorite passage from a book called *Power Through Constructive Thinking,* written by Emmet Fox, a scientist, philosopher, and spiritual teacher from the early 1900s:

### Your Heart's Desire (by Emmet Fox)

Already in your past life from time to time, God has whispered into your heart just that very wonderful thing, whatever it is, that He is wishing you to be, and to do, and to have. And that wonderful thing is nothing less than what is called Your Heart's Desire. Nothing less than that. The most secret, sacred wish that lies deep down at the bottom of your heart, the wonderful thing that you hardly dare to look at, or to think about—the thing that you would rather die than have anyone else know of, because it seems to be so far beyond anything that you are, or have at the present time, that you fear that you would be cruelly ridiculed if the mere thought of it were known—that is just the very thing that God is wishing you to do or to be for Him. And the birth of that marvelous wish in your soul—the dawning of that secret dream—was the Voice of God Himself telling you to arise and come up higher because He had need of you.

If you're struggling to uncover or express the wish of your soul, take heart! The first step in finding or doing work that you love is to create a life that you love. I promise you, if you do the exercises in this book, you will not only uncover the unique contribution you are destined to make in the world, but you will find it much easier to make.

Sometimes our talents and gifts are hidden beneath the clutter and debris of our lives, just waiting to be uncovered. Most people search prematurely for their "life purpose" or the work that they love. They wind up finding a temporary solution to a current problem in their life. For example, they think that an exciting new job will make up for the missing enthusiasm in a relationship. Or, because they need money, they agree to a job that pays well even though their talents and gifts will not be fully expressed. Remember this: doing the work throughout this book is the missing piece in discovering and doing work that you love.

## CELEBRATE YOUR SUCCESS!

As we come to the end of the coaching program, I'd like to congratulate those of you who have done the work outlined in this book. By changing your old behaviors and habits, you have created a higher-quality life. You've made incredible changes, and I'd like you to acknowledge and celebrate your success. Too often, those of us who take action and achieve what we set out to do move from one accomplishment to the next without stopping in between to notice how our lives have changed.

I'd like you to set aside an afternoon to review the work you've done throughout this book. How has your life changed? What inner and outer accomplishments have you achieved? It may be a tangible success, like the completion of your procrastination list or the improvement of your financial health, or a less tangible but equally important accomplishment, like a stronger connection with a loved one or less stress at work.

How have you grown? Are you more confident? Better able to set boundaries and say no? Do you automatically make decisions that honor your extreme self-care? Reflect on the way your life has changed and list twenty things that you are most proud of below:

1. _____
2. _____
3. _____
4. _____
5. _____
6. _____
7. _____
8. _____
9. _____
10. _____
11. _____
12. _____
13. _____
14. _____
15. _____
16. _____
17. _____
18. _____
19. _____
20. _____

Now look back over this list. Whether they are small or large changes, stop and notice the powerful impact each and every one has had on your life. Then, go one step further and share this list with your coaching partner or group. Hold a "bragging" party and listen carefully as each person shares his list and talks about how his life has changed.

How will you reward yourself? With the ongoing goal of strengthening your relationship with yourself, it's important to reward yourself for the changes you make. Give yourself a gift, take a day off, or schedule that trip you've always wanted to take. Some clients have even written letters to themselves acknowledging how they've grown. Do something special to fully appreciate your hard work.

Listing your accomplishments, the things you're most proud of, and rewarding yourself for them is a great exercise. Whether you use a date night, a soul retreat, or special event, make it a regular stop along the journey of your life.

———

As you continue to work this program and improve the quality of your life, you join a growing number of people who are strengthening their character and contributing to the world in a powerful way. You've probably noticed that your desire and ability to contribute to others has grown with each step you've taken throughout this program. A strong desire to contribute is an automatic response to a full, rich life.

The characteristics of those who live authentic lives demonstrate how powerful a contribution they are to others. These characteristics include the following:

- A willingness to take full responsibility for everything that happens
- A high level of integrity and a desire to continually raise the bar
- A belief that they are part of a greater whole and every action matters

- A strong commitment to serve others
- An enormous capacity for love and compassion

Wouldn't the world be a better place with more people like that? Stop and congratulate yourself for joining the ranks!

———

As your life starts to change and the magic starts to happen, people may call you lucky. Clients often smile when their friends and family tell them that they must have been born under a lucky star because of all the magical coincidences that just seem to happen. The truth is, anyone can be lucky if they're willing to do the work. Get started now! The life you were meant to live is waiting.

COACHING REMINDERS
*Work that you love follows a life that you love.*

- Review the Quality of Life checklist and do whatever it takes to create the life *you* want.
- Get creative! Find ways to make your work life add value to your whole life.
- Let your work be an expression of your unique gifts and talents.
- Celebrate your success! Reward yourself for your commitment and hard work—you deserve it!
- Most important—watch for the magic!

## RESOURCES

*BOOKS*

**Creating You & Company: Learn to Think Like the CEO of Your Own Career** by William Bridges (Reading, Mass.: Addison-Wesley, 1997)
This book walks the reader through a series of self-assessments and planning exercises in order to construct a successful career by thinking like the head of a small independent company supplying an employer.

**I Could Do Anything If I Only Knew What It Was** by Barbara Sher and Barbara Smith (New York: Delacorte Press, 1994)
This book helps readers discover what they really want and how to get it.

**Take Yourself to the Top** by Laura Berman Fortgang (New York: Warner Books, 1998)
A great book from America's #1 career coach. This book shows you how to leap out of a midcareer rut, identify obstacles that keep you from reaching your goals, honestly assess your career's progress, and more.

**Power Through Constructive Thinking** by Emmet Fox (HarperSanFrancisco, 1989)
A collection of thirty-one inspiring essays that show the reader how to have it all using the power of constructive thought.

**Finding Your Perfect Work: The New Career Guide to Making a Living, Creating a Life** by Paul Edwards and Sarah Edwards (New York: Putnam, 1996)
This book helps readers define what they really want in life and lists over sixteen hundred self-employment occupations.

**The Artist's Way at Work** by Mark Bryan, Julia Cameron, and Catherine Allen (New York: William Morrow, 1998)
The authors have adapted their techniques for fostering creativity as a means to spiritual fulfillment in the workplace.

**Doing Work You Love: Discovering Your Purpose and Realizing Your Dreams** by Cheryl Gilman (Contemporary Publishing, 1997)
Cheryl Gilman offers practical techniques and no-nonsense suggestions on everything from identifying the "right" job and networking to perfecting a résumé and interviewing.

**When Money Is Not Enough: Fulfillment in Work** by Eileen Hannegan (Beyond Words Publishing, 1995)
A guide to building healthy organizations and finding fulfillment in work.

**The Corporate Mystic** by Gay Hendricks and Kate Ludeman (New York: Bantam, 1997)
A guidebook for twenty-first-century leaders.

## MAGAZINES

**FAST COMPANY**
(800) 688–1545
www.fastcompany.com
Charter subscription, six issues for $14.95

**Work @ Home**
(800) 300–9828
www.workathomemag.com
Six issues for $18.95

## COACHING ORGANIZATIONS

**International Coach Federation**
(888) ICF–3131
www.coachfederation.org

**Coach University**
(800) 48–COACH
www.coachu.com

**Professional Coaches and Mentors Association**
(562) 799–2421
E-mail: PCMA@pacbell.net

# About the Author

CHERYL RICHARDSON is a personal coach who supports an international mix of corporate and individual clients who are committed to creating professional success without compromising their quality of life. She was the first president of the International Coach Federation and currently serves as the vice-chairman of the Interface Foundation. She is also a member of the Chief Executive's Club of Boston.

As a professional speaker, Cheryl has designed and presented programs to major universities, Fortune 500 companies, educational conferences, corporate workshops, retreats, and professional associations. Her work has been covered in numerous magazines and newspapers throughout the United States, and she has appeared on talk radio and television programs including *Donahue, Real Life, CBS This Morning,* and *Bloomberg Radio.* Cheryl lives in Newburyport, Massachusetts.

Her services include:
Individual Coaching
Group Teleconferencing Programs
Corporate Keynotes and
Workshops
Retreats

For her free online newsletter,
e-mail:
subscribe@cherylrichardson.com
Cheryl Richardson
P.O. Box 13
Newburyport, MA 01950
(978) 462–2204
E-mail: cheryl@
cherylrichardson.com